Yes We Can!

Advice on Traveling with an Ostomy
and
Tips for Everyday Living

Yes We Can!

Advice on Traveling with an Ostomy
and
Tips for Everyday Living

Barbara Kupfer
Kathy Foley-Bolch
Michelle Fallon Kasouf
W. Brian Sweeney, MD

YES WE CAN!
ADVICE ON TRAVELING WITH AN OSTOMY AND TIPS FOR EVERY-
DAY LIVING

ISBN 1-886284-59-8
Library of Congress Card Number: 99-069798
First Edition
ABCDEFGHIJK

Published by
Chandler House Press
335 Chandler Street
Worcester, MA 01602
USA

President
Lawrence J. Abramoff

Director of Publishing
Claire Cousineau

Editorial/Production Manager
James A. Karis II

Book Design
Michele Italiano-Perla

Cover Design
Alyson Levine and James Karis

Author Photos
Larry Stein

Chandler House Press books are available at special discounts for bulk purchases. For more information about how to arrange such purchases, please
contact Chandler House Press, 335 Chandler Street, Worcester, MA 01602,
or call (800) 642-6657, or fax (508) 756-9425, or find us on the World
Wide Web at www.chandlerhousepress.com.

Chandler House Press books are distributed to the trade by
National Book Network, Inc.
4720 Boston Way
Lanham, MD 20706
(800) 462-6420

For Our Families

Proceeds from the sale of this book benefit:

The United Ostomy Association
The American College of
Colon and Rectal Surgeons
The Worcester Ostomy Association

Foreword

The intent of this book is to serve as a useful and practical guide for the person who has an ostomy and wishes to travel. Whether you have recently had ostomy surgery or are a veteran, whether a seasoned traveler or a new adventurer, whether traveling across the state or out of the country, the pages that follow are filled with valuable tips for traveling.

My world-traveling patient, Barbara Kupfer, and I conceived this book after we realized no such guide was available. What follows then is useful information obtained from people around the world, presented in a format convenient for travel. Hopefully after reading this book you, too, will agree that "Yes, we can!"

Barbara, Kathy, Michelle and I have agreed to donate proceeds from the sale of this book to benefit the United Ostomy Association, The American College of Colon and Rectal Surgeons and the Worcester Ostomy Association.

—W. Brian Sweeney, MD

Authors' Notes

Traveling has always been part of my life, and when surgery for colon cancer was performed, I was determined to continue to "see the world." I had many questions about traveling with an ostomy, and although the ostomy associations and my medical caregivers were helpful, I felt there was a need for a definitive resource. If I was asking questions, then others were looking for answers too. I began to ask questions via the Internet and found that there were many persons with ostomies who had unique experiences and valuable knowledge to share. Kathy Foley-Bolch and I began to record this information, and as we worked, *Yes We Can* took on a life of its own.

—*Barbara Kupfer*

Since having ostomy surgery five years ago, I've been saddened by the number of people who have let this life-saving surgery have such a negative impact on their life. I've tried to help combat that, one person at a time, as a trained visitor for the Worcester Ostomy Association. In fact, that is how I met Barbara, who has really been the driving force behind this book. I wanted to be involved with this because I believe that the book has the potential to help so many get on with living, and because in this vehicle, we have the opportunity to reach so many more people, one at a time.

—Kathy Foley-Bolch

When Barbara and Kathy invited me to join the *Yes We Can* project, I was hesitant as I was still recovering from ileostomy surgery. I had a lot of questions about how I was going to cope with life-changing surgery and was concerned with returning to a full work and travel schedule, let alone participate in compiling a book! My fellow authors have shown me that I am able to do more now than I was ever able to do when I had Ulcerative Colitis. My thanks to my husband, mother, brother and to the doctors who have seen me through—Drs. David Rosenfield, Gary Wolf, Roger Epstein, Sidney Friedman, Joel Levenson and of course, Brian Sweeney.

—Michelle Fallon Kasouf

Acknowledgments

Linda and Ken Aukett—Linda and Ken contributed
sections of Chapter Four to *Yes We Can*. In addition,
Linda actively encouraged Barbara and Kathy to create this book.

✈

Julie Carr, RN—Julie contributed Chapters Ten and
Eleven to *Yes We Can*. Julie Carr: MS, RN, CETN is a
board certified enterostomal nurse, working in home
health care.

✈

Bobb L. Courtman is president of Medical—ID.com
and contributed the portion of Chapter Five that dis-
cusses medical jewelry. Bobb is the executive director
of the Internet Commerce Association.

✈

Louisa Corazzini, BS, RN, is a board certified enterostomal nurse, currently working in home health care. Louisa
contributed Chapters Ten and Eleven to *Yes We Can*.

✈

Micki Gelman is a freelance writer and contributing
editor for the *OSTOMY QUARTERLY*. Her work has
appeared in the *CINCINNATI ENQUIRER, ACCENT
ON LIVING* and other publications. She has a master's
degree in education administration and lives in Albu-
querque, NM, where she served as president of the
ostomy chapter, newsletter editor and support group
facilitator. Micki contributed to Chapter Five.

Janie Graziani is a freelance travel writer and manager of public relations for the American Automobile Association (AAA). Janie contributed travel expertise to Chapter Eight.

Kerry Ann McGinn, RN—Kerry contributed Chapter Seven to *Yes We Can*. Kerry is Nurse Practitioner specializing in Oncology. She has published several books, including *The Ostomy Book* and *The Ostomy Book for Nurses*.

Carol Norris—Carol contributed Chapter Nine to *Yes We Can*. Carol teaches writing at the University of Helsinki and has published several novels.

Gwen Turnbull RN, BS, CETN—Gwen contributed Chapter Four to *Yes We Can*. Gwen is a nurse registered in Pennsylvania and is in demand as a lecturer on ostomy and wound care. In addition to consulting, Gwen is a member of the Wound Ostomy Continence Nurses Society and the World Council of Enterostomal Therapists.

Mary Jane Wolfe taught mathematics at the junior and senior high school level for 12 years. She is currently managing editor for a major textbook publisher. Mary Jane has been active in UOA for about 25 years, and is now chapter president of the Ostomy Association of Boston. Mary Jane contributed Chapter Three to *Yes We Can*.

✈

Aliza Yaffe, RN—Aliza Contributed Chapter Five and part of Chapter Four to *Yes We Can*. Aliza is the head nurse of the Israel Cancer Association, in charge of the ostomy rehabilitation program, and was trained as an ET in Roswell Park Medical Center in Buffalo New York, was a board member of the WCET from 1990 to 1994, and chairperson of the WCET International Congress in 1996 in Jerusalem.

✈

Thanks to Jorgen Frey for his invaluable assistance in providing information on international ostomy supply sources.

✈

Thanks to Hollister Corporation for supporting the *Yes We Can* project, and its sponsorship of the Medical Identification Card included in the book and its help in creating bookmarks for our advertising effort. Thanks also to Jim Stupar of Hollister for his help in moving the *Yes We Can* project forward.

✈

Thanks to Cymed Corporation for its sponsorship of bookmarks in support of our advertising effort.

✈

Thanks to our travel story contributors: "Arne," Anne Favreau, Vladdimir Kleinwachter, Larry Trapp, Bob Rothschild, Petra and John van Vredendaal, George Salamy, Jorgen Kirk (Wiesent), Sharon Klein, Jorgen Frey, Jerry Gross, Gregory Haas, Pat Matranga, Jerry Greenberg, Velma Bragg, Denis Rush, Paul Morrison, Alice Kohn and family, Ingrid Johnson, Tom Sowerbutt, Crystal Scotti, Ron Titlebaum.

✈

Special thanks to Chandler House Press for its support, guidance and encouragement.

✈

Yes We Can! Advice on Traveling with an Ostomy and Tips for Everyday Living is a travel guide written by people from all over the world who are enjoying a renewed life after undergoing major surgery. This book depicts the true meaning and philosophy of the United Ostomy Association and its many local chapters. *Yes We Can* work, play, and certainly travel. This is the essence of what we in the UOA continually promote: Life doesn't stop after ostomy surgery and in most cases doesn't even slow down. The life of an ostomy patient can actually get better especially for those who have suffered for many years with the debilitating effects of diseases such as chronic Ulcerative Colitis or Crohn's disease. Ostomy surgery can not only save lives but it can actually provide a better quality of life. *Yes We Can*—enjoy a normal life.

As president of the Worcester (MA) Chapter of the United Ostomy Association, I am proud to support this book and I am especially proud that the authors are members of the Worcester Chapter.

—Bill Capman, President
Worcester Ostomy Association

Introduction

All methods of travel are open to you, and many people with ostomies are already traveling all over the world. Everything is possible, from cruises to safaris to camping to driving a tractor—trailer. People with ostomies are able to travel by land, sea, and air.

There are very few things that you will have to change when you prepare to leave home on your first adventure. For example, you should be aware of restroom accessibility, and adjust your food intake accordingly. You might want to avoid eating high—residue foods right before you leave. Try eating pancakes or a bagel for breakfast, rather than a bran muffin. Be aware of your body's digestive timing, and plan meals to avoid any potential problems.

Relax and Enjoy

I had ileostomy surgery in 1989 and since then I have traveled extensively through Europe, the US, Canada, Mexico, and cruised to the Caribbean. I have found that the only thing you need to do is use common sense, do not be negative, and have a good time! The first time I packed MEGA supplies and fretted, until I learned to relax and enjoy!

—Dan Tyrrell, President
United Ostomy Association

THE TRAVELLER by Ann Favreau

Six weeks after surgery,
Healing body, adventurous spirit,
On its way to New Zealand,
Stops to refresh on a fragrant Tahiti beach.
Pouch hidden beneath vibrant suit,
Dips into tropical water.
Barriers hold fast in the hot humid paradise.

Onward to winter on the other side of the world.
Flying away, a busman's holiday
Visiting schools down under.
Filling the void of disease with images
Pulsating with life.

Deer farms, trout pools,
A Glow worm Grotto twinkling in the dark
Of a crisp winter day.
Maori songs and Hangi feast illuminates the night.

Dairy farms without flies, litter—free byways.
School tots in stocking feet
With shoes outside the door.
Sheep dogs atop the flock
Dash to the tune of the whistler.
A topsy turvy view of life so far away from home.

I'm a traveler, a survivor,
Finding wonder in the ordinary.

—Reprinted from *The Healing Circle* by Ann Favreau

CHAPTER ONE

Twenty-Five Most Frequently Asked Questions

The following are twenty-five questions that we feel are most often asked by people anticipating their first (or twenty-first!) journey.

1. How soon after I have had ostomy surgery can I begin to travel again?

This depends entirely on how well you have recovered from the surgery, and the best people to help you with this are your medical team. We have known people who have traveled to the Caribbean within a month of having surgery, and we have known people who have had some complications and have had to stick closer to home for several months or more. It's all up to you and your doctor!

2. Are there any limitations to the distance that I can go?

How far do you want to go? Barbara Kupfer travels all over the world, whereas Kathy Foley-Bolch prefers to stay strictly within the confines of North America. These personal preferences have nothing to do with our ostomies. They are just those—personal preferences. Your limits are self-imposed.

3. Should I bring my own ostomy supplies?

Yes. We are always most comfortable with our own products, the appliances that we have become used to. (For more information, refer to Chapter Four).

4. What should I bring along? How much?

Figure out how many appliance changes you would normally use in the planned time period, then triple that amount. It's always a good idea to pack supplies in several different places in order to avoid problems should you lose or damage your luggage. You might want to divide your inventory of supplies with a traveling companion. (For more information, refer to Chapters Four and Five).

5. Will I be able to buy supplies while I'm away?

Yes, ostomy supplies are available throughout the world. Appendix IV provides information on many major supply houses around the world. This listing is intended to be a guide rather than a complete catalogue, and your health care providers may have alternate resources for you to contact. Closer to home, the Yellow Pages of most telephone books will give you the names of local suppliers. Be prepared to pay for emergency supplies out of your vacation funds, as most distant suppliers won't be able to accept your insurance for payment. Be sure to keep the receipt for any supplies purchased and turn it in to your insurer when you get home, as some insurance plans will allow reimbursement.

6. How often should I change my appliance while I'm away?

You should stick to the same basic routine you use when at home. Don't feel that you have to change it more often, and don't leave yourself open for problems by trying to break all records and not change it often enough. It's possible that new foods and schedules and other adventures could cause you to have to make a few adjustments, but you are the best judge of that.

7. How should I pack?

Always pack your ostomy supplies in your carry-on bags. It is not unusual to lose luggage. We suggest that you always carry a "spare" in your purse, briefcase, fanny pack or tote. Some manufacturers have great little zipper bags that can fit into a coat pocket as well. (For more information, refer to Chapters Four and Five).

8. Will my appliances be affected by the weather?

Heat and cold can cause the breakdown of your appliances. It is best not to leave them in the trunk or the glove compartment of your car for any extended periods of time. Some people recommend an insulated cooler or lunch bag to carry during your trip. (For more information refer to Chapter Four).

9. What if I need to clean my pouch, or irrigate? Is this going to be a problem for me when traveling?

If you cannot drink the water, then you shouldn't use it for cleaning your pouch, or for irrigation or anything else relating to your ostomy. We suggest that you buy bottled water in sealed containers from reputable vendors. (For more information, refer to Chapters Five, Six and Ten).

10. Should I wear a seat belt?

A seat belt is necessary on a plane, and is much safer for you when in a car. Your seat belt won't cause you any harm as long as it is adjusted comfortably. Some people use a clothespin and place it near the retraction slot in order to relieve any tension on the belt. There are also several different compa nies that manufacture seat belt shields if you feel more comfortable with that option.

11. Should I start my trip with a freshly changed appliance?

This is strictly a matter of personal preference, and there are pros and cons either way. We prefer to put on a new appliance the day before a trip, just to make sure that the seal is fine. You'll hear others say that it's best to change right before you leave, in order to LIMIT THE NUMBER OF CHANGES YOU EXPERIENCE while away from home.

12. How do I find a physician or ET Nurse?

The appendices feature a listing of American Society of Colon and Rectal Surgeons, the major associations of Wound and Ostomy Nurses and Enterostomal Therapists, along with the phone numbers of Ostomy Associations worldwide. In addition, there are reference telephone numbers and contact information on international physician referral agencies. If you have an emergency, contact your primary care physician if possible; otherwise go to the nearest hospital.

13. Do I need a medical card?

A medical card is not mandatory, but you will find one most helpful, especially if you are traveling out of the country. A medical card is included in this book.[1] The card we have provided has information about your ostomy,

[1] This medical card is sponsored by Hollister Corporation, manufacturer of ostomy supplies.

and will be especially helpful if you should be questioned in customs. If you do not choose to use the card, you should bring a note from your doctor, stating your condition and that you need to carry ostomy supplies and medications by hand.

14. Should I get a medical identification bracelet?

Medical identification bracelets, (also necklaces and tags) are a great idea, especially if something should happen and you are not able to speak for yourself. They're universally recognized, give medical personnel fast access to your records, and will minimize confusion about the type of ostomy you have. This type of jewelry is available from a variety of sources; see Appendix VI and Chapter Five for more details.

15. (a) When traveling by airplane, should I sit near the restroom?

That's another personal choice. If you feel more comfortable seated closer to the restroom, then it's a good idea. Anything that makes the trip easier for you is what you should do. You shouldn't have to empty your pouch more often than you normally do. An aisle seat is preferred by some in order to "beat the rush" after meal service. Additionally, a "Can't wait" card is available from Crohn's and Colitis Foundation of America,[2] which will help you move quickly through the line.

[2] Crohn's and Colitis Foundation of America contact information is featured in Appendix VI.

(b) Will air pressure changes in the airplane affect my appliance?

The short answer on the effects of air pressure is "no," your pouch will not inflate or "explode" when the air pressure changes in the airplane. For your own comfort, be aware of foods that give you gas; those foods will have the same effects when you are flying, and may cause your pouch to expand when you don't want it to.

16. Should I drink more fluids when traveling by air?

Yes. Pressurized air is much drier than normal and we suggest you drink at least twice the amount of fluids you would usually drink. It's important for you to stay hydrated while on the plane, so carry water with you. The servers offer beverages frequently, so use that as an additional reminder.

17. Will I have trouble passing through customs?

If an official notices a bulge, and wants to have you searched, you will find your medical card and/or doctor's note to be invaluable. Most people don't know what an ostomy is and a medical card or doctor's note will help to explain. The card may also help in your request for privacy if you are searched.

18. Which foods should I eat?

Try to stick with a diet as close to what you normally eat as possible. It's great to try native foods, but be cautious. Be especially wary about local fruits and vegetables; always wash them, using bottled water. Those with ileostomies should try to avoid high fiber foods that could cause a blockage. (For more information, refer to Chapter Six).

19. Can I travel with heavy luggage?

You should always be very careful about lifting heavy objects. Anyone who has had abdominal surgery is more susceptible to hernias, and you should follow your doctor's advice about how much weight you can safely lift. Be cautious about hitting your pouch with luggage and causing a puncture, hurting your stoma or disengaging the tail clip. Remember that no one has ever regretted traveling lightly!

20. What are some signs of being dehydrated?

One of the first signs is dry lips. If your lips start to feel dry, rest assured that you need to drink as soon as possible. Another way to test for dehydration is to pinch the skin on the back of your hand. If the skin does not spring back quickly and holds the "pinch" you are in need of fluids. Severe dehydration requires immediate medical attention. (For more information, refer to Chapter Eleven).

21. *What do I do if I become dehydrated?*

You need to drink, and get your electrolytes back in balance as soon as possible. Start drinking tea, sports drinks, and water (Barbara recommends chicken soup!). Also, salty snacks such as potato chips, saltines and pretzels will help you to retain fluids. More advanced dehydration could cause you to feel fatigued and disoriented; Do not let it get to this point, as you will require medical attention!

22. *Should I obtain travel insurance?*

It's a good idea to get travel insurance to cover any surprises like cancellations, lost luggage and medical emergencies. Talk with your agent before you leave home to find out if there are any exclusions you should be aware of. Before leaving home, confirm that your health insurance covers emergencies that are out of your coverage area, including emergency flights (and medical attendant care) to get you home. (For more information, refer to Chapter Eight).

23. *What happens if my appliance leaks or falls off while hiking or camping or on the plane or bus?*

It can happen, but it could happen at home too. Always bring an extra appliance and accessories with you in case of an "accident." Also, remember that very few places are so remote that you can't replace or clean soiled

clothing. Don't panic, take care of the problem, and get back to having fun.

24. How will I dispose of my used appliance while away?

There are many alternatives available to you,
but the easiest is probably a plastic shopping
bag, tied by the handles, and put in the trash.
Other options are several types of opaque self-
sealing bags that can be purchased from med
ical supply houses, baby diaper bags, or clear
sandwich bags with paper towels inserted.

25. (a) Should I consider swimming as recreation available to me?

This is such a commonly asked question that
we felt we had to address several aspects of
it. Yes, you can swim with an ostomy. The
pouch won't fall off, unless you are being buf-
feted by wave upon wave for hours in the salt
water. Kathy has gone swimming in the Bay
of Fundy and the cold Northern Canadian
Atlantic, and Barbara has frolicked in the
Mediterranean and the Red Sea. (For more
information, refer to Chapter Seven).

(b) Will people see my appliance?

They might, but in reality no one really
notices, and if they do, most people won't
know what they're seeing. But if it makes you
feel better, dark colors, textured fabrics and
patterns are more concealing; There are
many fabrics that stretch to help hold things

in place. Some women (and men) may find that wearing their underwear helps to conceal the appliance. Some men feel more comfortable wearing a tank style tee shirt when swimming to camouflage their surgery.

We hope these questions and answers have helped prepare you for traveling. All travelers must plan carefully. Pack your bags and hit the road!

So, when do you leave?

Chapter Two contains a few of the many stories about people who say, "Yes, we can." Most of the stories come from questions Barbara asked via the Internet. After her ostomy surgery, Barbara began to ask ostomy-related questions, especially about travel, that it seemed no one could answer locally. She was curious about what you do if you need to change an appliance, have a leak in the pouch, encounter problems with food, or any other experiences people with ostomies had. We chose the most exciting and educational of the stories that Barbara received. We hope these stories will help you decide that, yes you can, too!

STORY ONE

Kathy Foley-Bolch
Ileostomy, United States
"On The Road"

I had undiagnosed Ulcerative Colitis for many years. Once it was diagnosed in 1992, it progressively got worse no matter what the treatment, and on November 27, 1994, I had emergency surgery and woke up with a permanent ileostomy.

I had never realized that this was a cure for UC, and I was really surprised to have this new addition to my life. Fortunately, I had a strong support system that includes a wonderful husband and mother, and after a brief period of mourning and a hearty dose of self-pity, I got on with my life.

I had always been busy and active prior to getting sick, and it was important for me to get back to that type of lifestyle. It also made me realize that life is fragile, and nothing was going to hold me back.

When we first met, my husband taught me how to drive an 18-wheeler. We drove tractor-trailers across the country and eventually owned our own 48-state trucking company. As time went on, I gave up the driving and just handled the business end of the company while attending to other things. After I got sick, we sold the business, and my husband drove for a local company. Not knowing what to do after my surgery, we decided to try going back on the road as a team again. We traveled the Eastern US, and I found that I could do everything I did before. Truck stops have all the amenities one needs, and I was able to handle the ostomy with few problems. The biggest obstacle was getting into the truck after a fresh appliance change without dislodging the new appliance. Relaxing for an hour or so after a change helped the appliance to "set" and eliminated the problem. Before I learned that, I met some interesting people when I was forced to change in the men's room of a couple of warehouses. My husband would watch the door, but inevitably something would happen and he would be called away, and someone would walk in while I was "busy." Oh well.

The only other thing we did to simplify my life was to get a "porta-potty" so that I could stay in the truck at night, without having to get up when I had to empty the pouch. It was fun while it lasted, but we have since both moved on to other careers.

We also have a motor home, and travel as often as we can (traveling sure gets in your blood!). We tow a motorcycle or car behind us so that we can sample the local sites as we go along. One of the most interesting trips was to a wedding in Florida over Thanksgiving. We decided to just bring one motorcycle. My in-laws were having fits, because we were going to the wedding on the bike, and they were afraid of what I would look like. I wore a long satin shirt over leggings, and threw a satin broomstick skirt into the saddlebags. My hair is short and curly, so there was no problem with "helmet-head" and when we got to the church, I raced into the ladies room for a quick change, and no one was the wiser about our "chariot."

Probably the worst thing that happened to me on our trips was the blockage I got in Prince Edward Island after attending two of the local lobster suppers in a row. All the lobster and mussels didn't agree with my system, and I spent an uncomfortable night walking the aisle of the motor home while drinking hot sweet tea. I was lucky—the blockage cleared itself, and I learned to be a little more discreet with lobster meals!

As you can tell, the ostomy hasn't slowed me down a bit.

STORY TWO

"Arne"
Ileostomy, Norway
"An Artificial Kidney"

It was about 10 years ago, and I had had my ileostomy for about 15 years, and had made a lot of journeys. This special trip was only to Berlin, Germany, to visit one of the world's most famous fairs for electronics. At that time in my life I really had a problem with gas filling up my pouch rather rapidly and always at the most inconvenient times. The people of Berlin were still divided by the wall.

One afternoon just after a long day at the fair and after a fast food meal, I found myself standing in a long queue intending to visit East Berlin at the Friedrichsstrasse Station. The queue was long, and my stomach worked well, so it wasn't long before my pouch started to fill up. I was lucky not to be wearing tight jeans, so the disaster was not just around the corner, but I didn't feel too happy with the situation, as there were no toilets in the area.

Because the wall was still there, armed East German guards watched carefully everybody entering East Berlin. On this afternoon, an eager young guard, armed with a handgun, started to watch me carefully. Suddenly, I understood that the thing under my trousers was what he was observing! And then, after a couple of minutes, he came over and commanded me to follow him.

We went into a little side room and I had to undress. I guess you can imagine his astonished face when he saw my pouch and no handgun or grenade was present. I couldn't help asking him if he had seen such a thing before. "Nein, nein, no, no," he said.

"But do you know what it is?" I asked. This time he nodded eagerly, "Es ist eine kunstliche nure?" (It's an artificial kidney, isn't it?) he said.

Well, the wall is down, and I still wear my favorite brand of pouch, and Germany is Germany. Twice since my "artificial kidney" I have been searched at airports. Once an eager guard was checking under my trousers and he became so rough that it really hurt. For a short time I thought he would damage my little bowel-friend, but fortunately he stopped when I made it clear that it hurt me. So, friends, go ahead and travel the world, but take special care at border crossings!

STORY THREE

Ann Favreau, Vice President
United Ostomy Association
Colostomy, United States
"Practical Considerations and Hygiene"

I am Vice President of the UOA. I have done a great deal of traveling with a colostomy. After surgery in March of 1988, I traveled to Australia and New Zealand with a group of teachers. One of the best things that I brought with me was a small emptied hair-spray bottle. I put a small amount of detergent and water in it. It was helpful for cleanups in restrooms that had no water supply. Some bus facilities had no water either, only hand wipes. For foreign travel I still take it with me. The new antibacterial lotions can be a great aid. I always take more than enough appliance changes. I do not rely on trying to obtain supplies elsewhere. As you well know, one size does not fit all! It may be important to know that in places like Italy, you need to go into a restaurant, ice cream or coffee shop, or store to find a restroom. It is an accepted practice. In many countries there is a small fee that is paid before you enter restrooms in public areas. Even in highway gasoline stations that have food areas, there may be a matron at the door with her hand out. Keep the change of that country in hand.

If you are traveling with a group, it may be wise to tell the tour leader that you may have a restroom emergency so they don't leave you behind when you are in churches, museums, gondola rides and the like. It is easy to get confused if you are in an area that had many tour groups. Carry medication for diarrhea and motion sickness with you. You may never find a pharmacy when you need one. In remote areas the natives may not speak English. My husband did a fine acting job in a very small town trying to get me some motion sickness medicine after a bus ride down the Amalfi Drive in Italy. This was my first experience with it so I was unaware of this good rule of thumb: not to buy food from street vendors or eat raw fruit or vegetables. Hygiene may not be their number one concern. In Guatemala we saw street children refilling water bottles from the public well and selling them to tourists. You obviously need to keep yourself well hydrated, but be cautious about where you obtain the bottled water. I hope these suggestions will help.

STORY FOUR

Dr. Vladdimir Kleinwachter
Ileostomy, Czech Republic
"Travel After Several Surgeries"

I had problems with ulcerative colitis in my youth. After unsuccessful conservative therapy the physicians decided to make a caecostomy to relieve the large intestine, but this was again without success. Instead of improving the intestinal state, it completely degenerated and had to be removed. It was possible to save a part of the rectum and to make an ileorectal anastomosis. I lived with it for nearly 12 years without any complications, but then a tumor developed in the rectum and it was necessary to make a terminal ileostomy. This happened in 1973 and reliable appliances were available. I had to have the stoma re-operated on several times, and thus its surroundings are not ideal. I have several deep scars near the opening. In spite of that, I do not feel too many limitations. I travel, hike, ski and have tried paragliding.

When traveling I always use two-piece appliances. They can be kept in place five or six days. I take a sufficient reserve of appliances with me. Because of the scars in the stoma vicinity, I put microporous tape around the flange and cover it with normal surgical tape in the critical areas. If the flange starts to leak, this will keep the moisture in for awhile. I use a belt, and without it I do not feel safe. I wear rather loose underpants into which I have sewn an inner pocket for the pouch. It serves as insulation against sweating, supports the pouch when it is too full and heavy, and in case of an unpleasant accident, it prevents the pouch contents from leaking out for awhile.

If I travel under more primitive conditions (such as with a tent) I change the appliance whenever I find suitable conditions. I eat only meals that do not cause problems for me. This is very individual, and everybody must experiment to determine what is good for him or her. As prevention for flatulence, I take a Czech-made anti-flatulence drug every day. I carry an over-the-counter medication to use in case of diarrhea.

Of course, I have experienced several disastrous situations, but after a long life with a stoma I became somewhat obdurate. For example last year, when I was hiking in the mountains, the pouch clip opened in a very unsuitable place on a narrow ridge. I had to undress in an open place, with people walking around, and wash everything using only a bottle. I closed the pouch, wrapped my abdomen in plastic, and continued.

Connie Thompson
United States
"Traveling with a Bag Bomb!"

Do you remember making bag bombs when you were a child? You know, the mixture of water, vinegar and baking soda in a zip-lock bag, that would start smoking and then explode and if you were really lucky, the bag would make a mess when it exploded. But if you didn't follow the instructions carefully, and didn't pay attention to the smallest details, your bag bomb wouldn't bomb, you would just have a bag full of water, vinegar and baking soda.

By now you may be wondering what on earth bag bombs have to do with traveling and having an ostomy. Maybe nothing, but I think they are the perfect thing to use when describing an ostomy bag. With a bag bomb, you have to pay attention to the small details so it will bomb. With an ostomy bag, you have to pay attention to the small details so it WON'T bomb.

I have a 10-year-old who has an ileostomy and a continent urinary diversion (a

Mitrofanoff Channel placed through the umbilicus to make it possible to catheterize). Has her ostomy bag ever turned into a bag bomb? Yes. Did it ruin her trip? No. Does her ostomy slow down her travels? No. Does it restrict where she travels? No. Does it restrict the mode of transportation she chooses? No. She travels everywhere. She travels by car, train, plane, and even horse. However, if she doesn't pay attention to the small details, her ostomy bag will turn into a bag bomb.

So she travels everywhere; Traveling is the easy part. But does she go camping? I bet a child can't go camping if she has an ostomy. Oh, yes she can and does go camping. So she goes camping. I bet she can't go to sleep-away summer camp. Yes she can, and yes she does. Ok, so she goes camping, and she goes away to summer camp, but I bet she can't participate in all the activities. Yes she can, and yes she does. Ok, but I bet she doesn't go swimming. Yes she can, and yes she does.

Not only does she swim, but she dives from the high-dive. And she water skis, and jet skis and rides horses and rock climbs and does obstacle courses. How is all this possible? A child with an ostomy can't possibly swim, or ski, or rock climb. Yes she can, as long as attention is paid to the small details.

What small details am I referring to? I am referring to always having plenty of supplies available and that they are stored properly. I am referring to making sure the supplies are used properly. The wafer is securely attached to the skin. The bag is securely hooked onto the flange. The bag is in good repair. The bag has been emptied prior to beginning the activity. No little holes for contents to leak through. If swimming is the scheduled activity, paying attention to the small details includes securely attaching a closed-end pouch to the flange and taking the time to frame the wafer with waterproof tape.

The key to successful traveling and keeping your child's ostomy bag from becoming a bomb is paying attention to the small details. As a parent of an ostomate, I have quickly found that five minutes worth of pre-travel prep can prevent 60 minutes worth of post-travel bag bombs. I have learned from hands-on experience that if you leave the house, even if it's for a five minute run to the corner store for a soda, with no extra supplies, and without insisting that the ostomy bag be emptied, you will have the perfect makings for a bag bomb. On the flip side, if your child empties the bag prior to leaving the house, and has filled a backpack with enough supplies for every member of the United Ostomy Association, your travels will be uneventful.

Humor from the mouth of a child:

Said to a doctor who told her he needed to do a rectal exam: "That is an EXIT, not an entrance."

Said to an x-ray tech who was preparing to do a barium enema: "With friends like you, who needs an enema?"

Said to her urologist: "After my surgery, why don't you just tattoo 'No Service Either Exit' on my butt?"

STORY SIX

Bob Rothschild
Urostomy, United States
"Attitude"

I don't travel a lot with my ostomy. I have had some minor mishaps, but they happened at home and were no big deal. It seems to me that the real bad things happen to people with a bad attitude. I believe it was the skater Scott Hamilton who said when he was stricken with cancer: "The only disability in life is a bad attitude." I have always subscribed to that motto and in any difficult situation have looked for the lighter side to relieve the anxiety. So I found something comical to grin at after my surgery, the removal of my bladder and prostate one and a half years ago.

I was supposed to go to the hospital on the Friday after the weekend of our nephew's wedding. But on the Friday before the wedding I received a call from the hospital to report on Monday. No mention was made of any restrictions. The wedding was a big event and on Monday morning, in preparation for the surgery, it took six enemas to clean me out. It was not pleasant, but I found it funny and anticlimactic.

Another motivation, which has pulled me through many predicaments, is this: I am a survivor of World War II. When I find myself in a difficult situation, I think of the millions of victims and those who died fighting. Every one of them I am sure would gladly change places with me. It has always worked and it has helped me overcome many difficult situations.

STORY SEVEN

John van Vredendaal
Colostomy, Holland
"Traveling to Nepal"

My name is John van Vredendaal. I am Dutch and lived for one year in Seattle when I was 20. Two years after I came back to the Netherlands I was operated on and had a colostomy on the large intestine. So, I was 23 years old and still wanted to travel a lot. A good test to start was Nepal. My then girl-friend (now wife) Petra and I wanted to do a budget tour with one week hiking in the Himalayas. We did not know what to expect. I thought, "When I survive this trip in a good way, then there is no limit for traveling." And

I was right.

First of all, as an ostomy patient, you can take 12 Kilos (over 25 pounds) extra luggage, but when you go backpacking, 12 Kilos is all you want to take. So we had to be very smart about packing the backpacks. We bought a lot of super-light gear, like sleeping mats, sleeping bags, etc. I did not have any trouble trekking through Nepal at all. Actually, I have never been happier with my colostomy, after Petra told me how the toilets looked. The toilets were just a pit in the ground, with all the deposits of the trekkers who were there before. I simply went into the woods and changed my bags. Sometimes I had to dump them in the woods, but most of the times there were dumpsters. The only problem was it was sometimes difficult to find clean water to clean my colostomy. Oh, and diarrhea was not a problem either. It was just a matter of changing the bags in time, but I did not have to run to the closest "rest room."

Two years later we went to Ecuador. We visited the jungle and the Galapagos Islands. No problem! Last year we went to Egypt— same story.

Travel agents organized all these trips. Now we are planning to go on our own to Vietnam. This will take a bit of extra planning and organizing, but we will have a good time!

STORY EIGHT

George Salamy
Ileostomy, United States
"Common Sense"

I have been an ileostomate for 22 years and have traveled around the world for my company. I have been to more than 20 countries including many in the Middle East and the Far East. Though many countries were "up to par," many were not. But you survive.

Some helpful hints:

Regarding the amount of supplies, bring the supplies that you think you will need, and then double the amount.

Bring a list of suppliers in the area you are traveling to, or if possible, get a contact of someone in the area who is familiar with the dealers AND doctors.

Once in an emergency, when my supplies ended up going somewhere else with my suitcase (never check your supplies with your bags), I called the emergency room in a local hospital and they were willing to give me an appliance from their pharmacy until mine arrived.

Don't stop traveling for fear of your ostomy and the appliances!

Use COMMON SENSE when traveling—You'll have a ball.

STORY NINE

Jorgen Kirk
Urostomy, Denmark
"Travel in Africa"

I have had a urostomy since I was 15 years old. Although many people have problems with leakage, I have had fewer than 10 problems. I only change bags once a week—a half-hour in the bathroom and I will go for another week without thinking about it. I go on vacation often, and even six hours swimming does not cause problems for me.

I am a press photographer and my free time is spent hunting and traveling with my wife and daughters. We have gone to Canada, Norway, Malta, Spain and Sweden and recently returned from a safari in Namibia. It was very hot there (lots of thorny bushes too) but I had no problems with leakage and changed bags as I regularly would. We chose to go to Namibia because it has a good health system. We stayed at a farm that had private bath and toilet facilities.

When you travel, you always forget something from home and I forgot the hanger for my bags. I use a hanger after I have washed the bags so that the bags dry quickly—but the hanger was at home. Luckily, there was a curtain for the shower and so I removed the hanger for the curtain and used it for my bags. The next day when the maid came out from cleaning our room, she looked at me in a strange way. I had forgotten to pack the bag and it was still hanging where the shower curtain should be! Again I must say that I am a lucky ostomate; I live a completely normal life *with* my ostomy and not *for* it.

What I bring:
- ✔ Paste.
- ✔ Paste Remover.
- ✔ Tape.
- ✔ Powder.
- ✔ Soap to wash the bags.
- ✔ A small flashlight (in case the electricity goes out).
- ✔ A new elastic belt (ostomy belt).
- ✔ Some prescriptions in case of infection.

Some further advice:
- ✔ Trust your judgment and trust your bags.
- ✔ Bring what you need and a little extra.
- ✔ Never let your ostomy supplies out of your sight.
- ✔ Split your inventory of supplies between yourself and your traveling companion.
- ✔ If you do ask another person to carry supplies for you, make sure that you each have enough supplies to cover your needs for the entire trip, in case one of you loses luggage.

✔ Pack all your supplies in your carry-on luggage.

✔ Talk to your doctor before you go.

✔ Research the country you are traveling to—including the availability of medical help and ostomy supplies.

✔ Get good travel insurance.

STORY TEN

Velma Bragg, RN, CETN,
BCIR, United States
"Traveling with a Continent Ileostomy"

Today, when someone is facing the removal of their colon and rectum, there are three viable surgical procedures available. They are the standard Brooke Ileostomy, the Ileoanal Reservoir (IPAA, J Pouch) and the Continent Ileostomy (Continent Intestinal Reservoir: Kock or Barnett CIR). The Brooke procedure was introduced in the early 1950s followed by the Kock pouch in the 1960s, and the Ileoanal reservoirs and the Barnett modification in the late 1970s.

So, *Yes We Can* make a choice as to which procedure we have according to our underlying diagnosis and the one that perhaps best suits our lifestyle. It is important for the physician, patient, significant other and perhaps the ET nurse to discuss in detail all possible options, explore these options and decide which surgical choice is appropriate for that individual.

After suffering with Ulcerative Colitis for 10-plus years, I faced ileostomy surgery and had a standard Brooke ileostomy in 1977. I lived a rather successful life for 8 1/2 years with my external pouch. Already a registered nurse, I became obviously more interested in ostomy surgery and outcomes by entering the ET Nursing program in 1980 (now known as Wound, Ostomy and Continence Nurse—WOCN) and became certified in my nursing specialty. With my ostomy knowledge base enhanced and with the assistance of my surgeon, I learned of the ileostomy options with a trend toward continence. In 1985 I converted to the Barnett Continent Intestinal Reservoir procedure and what a difference it made in my life. I again had control of a bodily function that I had lost. The Brooke was wonderful compared to UC. It freed me of pain and suffering, and allowed me to return to many normal activities of daily living. But I had lost control of elimination of fecal waste, which necessitated wearing the external pouch as a collection device.

I am in control of bowel elimination by inserting a catheter through a small stoma and into my internal reservoir two to four times a day usually at my convenience. There are no limitations to activities or clothing. I need only wear a small absorptive pad to contain the mucous from the stoma. Of course, the catheter becomes the item that will be my sidekick for life! No pun intended.

Yes We Can, enjoy travel, the beach, food, sports, recreation and like others, just make the most out of God's gift of life. I would like to discuss several considerations when planning a trip or traveling with a continent ostomy. As with any vacation, trip, or simply a walk in the park, careful planning and preparation is the key for a successful endeavor.

CATHETER: Large bore #30 Silastic catheter (Mentor™, Medcna™, Marlen™). This catheter is similar to your American Express™ card: "Don't leave home without it!" For out of town or longer trips, plan to take several different sizes and kinds of catheters with you in the event you experience difficulty intubating. This is especially important if you are traveling out of the country. If you forget your catheter you can go to any local hospital, large or small, and most pharmacies—which will usually have a variety of Foley™ or straight catheters. Over the years, I have heard of all sorts of places where catheters are kept on a daily basis as well as when traveling. Men are known to coil the catheter and place it in their sock, in their coat pocket or pants pocket. Also a toothbrush holder is a useful tool to hold your catheter and place it in a pocket. The fashionable "fanny pack" is an excellent bag to carry supplies. A zip top bag is often used by both men and women in which to place a soiled catheter until they can get to a private area to cleanse the catheter. It may be somewhat easier for a female since most of us will have a purse of some sort. A small pouch such as a small makeup container is often used to place necessary items such as a plastic wrap with catheter, a dressing and perhaps some sort of lubrication. There is a lubrication wipe available that is an easy take-along. I usually take a small bottle of room deodorizer to spray at the time of intubation or strike a match to diminish the fecal odor. However, I always notice that non-ostomy persons just "do it" and go on about their business. It is also nice to take a candle to light in the bathroom. Especially if you are staying overnight as a guest in someone's home or in a hotel where you are sharing a room with someone. There are also deodorizing tablets to take internally if you desire. The catheter, post-intubation, is cleansed with just plain soap and water. Understand that this is not a sterile procedure and the use of caustic chemicals to cleanse or try to sterilize the catheter could cause a chemical reaction within the pouch. If I am in a public place such as an airport bathroom, I will flush the toilet as normal and then flush the second time while holding my catheter at the stream of water entering the commode, which will initially flush out the catheter. The catheter is then wrapped in toilet tissue and while I am washing my hands, the catheter is being cleansed at the same time and no one even notices what I am doing. If there is a diaper change area available, I will use it. Intubation on an airplane is a breeze. Everything you need is within arm's distance.

INTUBATION: The process of draining the reservoir using a catheter when the patient gets a full feeling in the pouch area. Simply lubricate the cath tip with a water-soluble lubricant, mineral oil, tap water or even mucous from the stoma and access valve. Slowly introduce the catheter into the reservoir through the stoma and allow the pouch to drain into commode or other collecting receptacle. Remember to always direct the end of the catheter toward the collecting receptacle before you enter the pouch. The pressure sometimes within the pouch can cause a splash. Also if you fanfold toilet tissue into the commode it will break the splash. If you meet resistance or have difficulty, gently apply pressure to the catheter while gently advancing it into the pouch and breathing deeply. NEVER FORCE THE CATHETER. The process of draining the pouch takes from three to five minutes. If the consistency of stool is too thick, increase fluid intake of grape juice or a glass of wine. It may also be helpful to dilute the contents by irrigating with a syringe of tap water. Remember to never insert anything in your pouch that you would not put in your mouth! It may also be helpful to irrigate the pouch once daily to rid it of any residual bacteria that could possibly cause pouchitis. This is done by inserting one to two ounces of tap water into the pouch and allowing it to drain back out. Repeat a couple of times. Pouchitis is an inflammation within the pouch with no known etiology. It produces diarrheal-type stool that will require more frequent intubation, but responds to antibiotics in most cases. Not all pouch patients have pouchitis but it is a possibility of all fecal pouch procedures be it a BCIR or J-Pouch.

INTUBATION RESISTANCE: If there is a problem intubating or if you meet resistance, try the following prior to "panic" or calling a physician or ET nurse:

Use a smaller catheter. Be sure to return to your usual catheter once pouch is successfully drained. Continued use of smaller catheter may result in stoma shrinkage with inability to use larger catheter. The larger catheter is designed to accommodate consistency of ileal output and to quicken the emptying process.

Try a different body position to intubate. If you have been sitting on the toilet, try lying down, kneeling or standing.

Relax, breathe deeply or even remove catheter and return later to try again.

Try inserting water or mineral oil in syringe through the catheter while advancing catheter.

Call a friend who has a mature continent

diversion and ask for assistance or suggestions.

If the pouch is full and you have tried all of the above suggestions unsuccessfully, call your physician or health care professional. If you are experiencing problems with intubation and you are away from your health care environment, use a soft #28 Foley™ catheter and leave it in the pouch until you can contact your physician. Tape it in place and you may connect it to a leg bag or clamp it between intervals of draining. ALWAYS cut away the inflatable balloon on end of catheter. Never inflate the balloon in Foley™ catheters that are used with a CIR as it may cause undesirable pressure on the valve.

DRESSINGS: Use a small absorptive bandage to contain mucous drainage from stoma. Remember if traveling to take a supply to last for your entire trip. There is a commercially manufactured patch that has an absorptive pad with waterproof tape. Or you may use panty liners or feminine pads cut in small squares with adhesive strips adhered to undergarment and absorptive area over stoma. Heavy-duty paper towels, 2x2 gauze or even toilet tissue with waterproof tape are all used. Each individual has a varying amount of mucous drainage and will use whatever is suitable to each person's needs. If you produce an excessive amount of mucous, you might consider taking an anti-histamine or decongestant medication. A dressing is not necessarily needed while swimming. The mucous will only cause a "wet spot" on an already wet swimsuit.

SKIN CARE: Peristomal skin irritation is not usually a problem. No feces will be on the skin because the feces exit through the catheter. The mucous drainage on the dressing will sometimes produce a yeast appearance from the sustained moisture to the area. This can be prevented by the use of a skin sealant wipe that leaves a plastic-like covering around the stoma protecting the skin. Skin care creams may be used when the condition occurs and also to maintain a healthy environment of tissue. There are also medicated creams and powders to treat the yeast if symptoms persist. More frequent dressing changes may be necessary where there is a large amount of mucous drainage.

DIET: As with any person who has an ostomy, it is always advisable to chew food thoroughly. With the CIR, undigested food particles can occlude the catheter making it difficult to drain. When this happens, you must remove the catheter, clean out the tube blockage, reinsert the catheter and continue to drain. There is no physical harm done but it will require a longer intubation process. If we want the food badly enough, most of us will eat it and know that we are going to take longer in the bathroom. This differs from food blockage in the Brooke ileostomy. With the Brooke, the undigested blockage usually is within six to eight inches of the stoma and causes an obstruction of the small intestines. The bolus of blockage is unable to exit through the stoma. In the CIR, the undigested particles are within the pouch and will exit only when the catheter is introduced to drain the pouch. They become stuck within the catheter on exit and the catheter is simply cleaned and reintroduced.

In summary, remember the following tips when traveling with a continent intestinal reservoir or maintaining daily activities:

✈ Keep your catheter available. Keep extra cath in vehicle, boat, office, and vacation cabin/home. Never pack your catheter, ostomy supplies or medications in your checked luggage.

✈ If water purification is questionable, use bottle water to drink, brush teeth, irrigate pouch and to clean catheter. Three ways to purify water:

Ten drops chlorine bleach to one quart of water; let stand thirty minutes prior to use.

Five drops of 2% Tincture of Iodine to ten drops of clear water added to one quart of water.

One to two Hallzone™ tablets added to one quart of water.

✈ Be careful when trying new foods while away on an extended trip.

➤ Consult your physician prior to visiting a foreign country and prepare medication kit to prevent suspected illnesses. Take anti-diarrheal and other medications with you in your carry-on luggage.

➤ Changes in normal routines may be interrupted when traveling in different time zones.

➤ Teach someone else to intubate your pouch in the event you are unable to perform the task.

➤ Always wear or have present a letter from your doctor, or medical identification jewelry indicating your type of ostomy and the telephone number for assistance.

➤ Educate your hometown physician and other health care professionals that may be seeing you in an emergency situation.

STORY ELEVEN

Sharon Klein
BCIR, United States
"Adventures with a BCIR"

I am 41 years old and I have a Barnett continent intestinal reservoir (BCIR), which I have had for 10 years as a result of 7 1/2 years of ulcerative colitis. I am a very active person and enjoy traveling. The trips my husband and I take are not what you would call conventional. I love to sea kayak, hike, camp, fish, and do both downhill and cross-country skiing.

When I first received my BCIR the first question I asked was if I would have to change my lifestyle. I was told that there were only two things I couldn't do—climb Mount Everest and scuba dive past 100 feet.

Since having surgery, I have traveled to such exotic locales as Belize, Guatemala, Baja, and the San Juan Islands in Washington state and Alaska. All trips have been camping and kayaking, and at times I was more than 50 miles from the nearest hospital or bathroom facility. During these trips, I have discovered different ways to make traveling easier.

Thank goodness for zip-lock bags! They are a BCIR patient's best friend, and the first thing I pack! I make up an intubation set using a gallon zip-lock bag. I put in several smaller zipper bags (three or four per day for each day away from bathroom facilities), a couple of packets of tissues, some pre-moistened wipes, a small bottle of antibacterial hand cleaner, and a collection of tubes (never, ever throw out a tube!) The extra tubes are just in case I can't wash my tube out, or I'm not near facilities. When I need to intubate, I put one end of the tube into the zip bag, and close the bag as much as possible, and intubate with the other end. When done, I remove the tube, put it in the zip bag, and close the bag. I now have a leak proof and odor proof bag that can be deposited in the nearest trash receptacle. I then sanitize my hands with the waterless cleaner. This works in the middle of nowhere, but is also great in the car when I've been stuck in traffic.

Another problem I have faced in the wilderness is irrigating. I don't irrigate often, but sometimes when I'm away I find that I tend to run thicker than usual. As most BCIR and continent ileostomy recipients can attest, you need two hands and a water supply to irrigate, as well as something to keep the water in. Once while camping in Alaska, I ate some food that clogged the tube. I was at a base camp with a makeshift porta-potty (a bucket with a toilet seat on it). It was fine for intubating, but I had to figure out how to irrigate. I finally took an empty water bottle and cut off the top with a knife, then poked holes in both sides of it, and ran a string through it. I filled the bottle with water and hung it from a nearby branch and used it as a well to fill my irrigation syringe (another thing I never leave home without!). I always bring a water bottle with a squirt top. The pressure from squeezing it is perfect for rinsing out a tube. Just make sure to remember which is for rinsing and which is for drinking.

STORY TWELVE

Jorgen Frey
Denmark
"Travel Cards and Saunas"

When traveling I bring my own ostomy
equipment. I also bring a list of addresses of
dealers in different countries that I got from
my supplier so I can buy my usual equipment
if I run out of bags, etc. The problem is that
there are only dealers in more "civilized"
parts of the world. Another thing to take into
consideration is that ostomy equipment for
Danish citizens living in Denmark is paid for
by the public (local county authority), in
accordance with the social laws. Even if you
have a very high income, the public pays for
your equipment; why buy abroad when you
can get it free of charge at home?

When I am traveling abroad I bring my
Stoma-Card[3] with me. On the card is written:
"The card holder has had an ostomy operation. The luggage contains bags and products for the treatment of the stoma as well as
required medical supplies. For human reasons please carry out customs check or other
examination of the luggage discreetly. Doctor's name and stamp (signature) can be
found on the reverse." The text is printed in
English, Danish, German, French, Russian,
Japanese, Chinese, Arabic, Indian and
Finnish. This card has been of great help to

[3] A medical card is included in this book. See card for instructions.

me, and the customs officers I have encountered all over the world have always followed the above-mentioned guidelines.

When flying, I always take a sponge bag in my hand luggage containing two ring plates (wafers), nine bags, cotton balls, a small mirror (to help me place the appliance), lotion, scissors, and hand towels. I have often changed bags while in flight, especially when going to Australia—a 20-hour trip. Food on airplanes has never been a problem; I am able to eat and drink what is served on board.

I am never afraid of traveling and when I am well prepared, I never give my ostomy a thought. The only time I did not know how to handle a situation was when I was invited to lecture at a conference in Finland. The conference was held at an estate that had a sauna. Part of the social aspect of the conference was to have an evening sauna and beer. I spent the day trying to figure out how to avoid the sauna and came to the conclusion that I should just tell the truth about my ostomy. Everyone accepted my excuse for not participating in the sauna bath, but I had the impression that the other conference participants did not know how to handle the situation!

STORY THIRTEEN

Jerry Gross
BCIR, United States
"Tips for Traveling with a BCIR"

My experience traveling with a BCIR has really been so much better than traveling with the ileostomy that I had previous to the BCIR. I have no problems with embarrassing leakage problems or having my pouch swell up from gas and having to always carry something to hide it until I make it to a bathroom. I had a conversion from an ileostomy to a BCIR in January 1988. Since that time, I have had virtually no problems at all. It has changed my life.

Dr. Barnett did my surgery. The BCIR stands for Barnett Continent Ileostomy Reservoir. I was so pleased that he helped so many people like me before passing away. His favorite saying was: "Whatever It Takes." He was so right.

I only take a small, flat zippered case (you can find them at many stores) with my catheter and a small container (empty sample bottle will do) of mineral oil for times when inserting the catheter is a problem. I keep this in my purse always. I use the catheter, flush the toilet and then reflush to clean the catheter. If you wish, when you return home, clean the catheter in hot soapy water.

I always have an extra catheter in another zippered case in my car just in case I change my purse and forget to put it in. It's always there for emergencies.

When traveling on vacation, I always take my bottle and syringe for irrigating. I do this every night no matter what. I believe that has been what has kept me from having pouchitis. I have had only two bouts with this in 10 years. TIP: Purchase disposable diapers, cut them into about five sections and tape the ends with some surgical tape or some kind of hypoallergenic tape. The patch is flesh colored and only about four inches by four inches in diameter. I also order an extra absorbency pad to go in the small hole in the patch. It's just another precautionary measure. I also have made my own covering using cloth diapers. They are nice for wearing around the house and can be washed and used over and over again.

STORY FOURTEEN

Jorgen Frey
Denmark
"Saudi Arabia"

Because of the heat in Saudi Arabia, traveling with an ostomy can be a bit complicated. A normal, flexible ring plate will leak because of the extreme heat if it is not changed every day; the alternative is a non-flexible ring plate, which has a bigger area to adhere to the skin. Unfortunately non-flexible ring plates are not as comfortable as the flexible ones. Before I left Denmark, I obtained non-flexible ring plates and got addresses of ostomy supply houses in Jeddah and Riyadh, although there were no referrals available for ET nurses. The medical system in the larger cities in Saudi Arabia is excellent.

STORY FIFTEEN

Jerry Greenberg
Colostomy, United States
"Substitute Equipment"

I am 74 years old and have had a colostomy for 24 years. Prior to retiring I had a job that required both domestic and foreign travel. I have managed to irrigate in many different situations, often under less-than-ideal conditions but always accomplished a satisfactory result. Since retiring, I have gone on many trips, including countries that range from Ireland to Australia. My wife and I have just completed a 24-day freighter trip from Sydney, Australia, to Long Beach, California, and I did not miss a single irrigation.

I had one experience that fortunately turned out fine but at the time it happened I thought it might be a disaster. I had visited my daughter, who lives in Long Island, New York, prior to going to a United Ostomy Association conference in Pittsburgh. I irrigated while visiting my daughter and left my irrigation equipment hanging in her bathroom to dry, as I wanted it to be dry when I packed it.

We left for the conference the next morning. When it came time to irrigate, I realized that the water supply pouch was not in my bag of ostomy equipment. It was evening and all of the ostomy suppliers were closed. The only place open that I could find was a nearby drug store. I went there but they had no ostomy supplies so I purchased a hot water bottle with an enema attachment. I was able to use it with some difficulty to achieve a fairly good irrigation. The next day I called my supplier in Ohio since I knew they would be exhibiting at the conference. I was lucky to learn that their representatives had not yet left for the show. I ordered a kit that they brought with them. They arrived later that day and I had the pouch in time for my next irrigation.

STORY SIXTEEN

Denis Rush
Colostomy, Northern Ireland
"Body Searches"

I am from Northern Ireland and I have had my colostomy for several years. At home we are regularly stopped and searched by British soldiers or police. I received my colostomy as a result of being injured in a terrorist attack on my home in which I was badly wounded. Being body searched can be embarrassing when strangers put their hands on your body and you know they don't know what to expect. I have been asked, "What's this?" and I have tried to tell them quietly "It's a colostomy." I don't know whether they do this deliberately or not, but on occasions they have said very loudly, "IT'S A WHAT?" and by this time I have gone completely red in the face—you can imagine it is not very pleasant.

Thank God there is relative peace in Ireland now and searches do not happen so often. I also have had problems at airports where you also have to go through searches. My life was not very happy and I did not go out of doors for a long time but I have had to come to terms with these circumstances I find myself in. Life must go on.

STORY SEVENTEEN

Paul Morrison
Ileostomy, United States
"Traveling in China and the US"

My biggest problem, or challenge, was in public toilets in China, where the men's room has dividers just a few inches high with square toilets. The first one I went in I looked then put off using it until I couldn't wait any longer. I thought the Chinese would think these Westerners really strange, emptying a pouch. But the Lord looks after us; no one came in while I was there!

Another time, in the US, we were camping our way around the country and were in a campground in Kentucky. I was going to change my appliance in the main bathroom, since it wasn't convenient in our pop-up trailer. I removed the old appliance, then discovered I had not taken any water for washing in the booth. So, I masked my stoma with tissues, rushed across the entire width of the converted barn, got water and returned to complete the job.

Another time in a campground, it was hot and sticky, but I put off showering because the community shower room had no dividers and four open showers. But I was so uncomfortable I finally took my three sons in with me. They finished quickly and left so I decided I was going to tell anyone who came in and asked that it was my money pouch, since it cost $10,000 in 1959. But, no one came in, and I was conditioned for public appearances *au naturel*.

About six months after my surgery I went water skiing and did better than I ever had before. I have had only one problem with water skiing—I don't own a boat and have to wait until someone invites me. I have also gone backpacking with my sons, beginning when I was 50 years old. We had some great times, but they grew up and left the old man at home while they went off on much more exciting trips around the country.

My wife doesn't have an ostomy, but she is a retired RN and has had lots of experience nursing ostomies of all kinds, including mine. We will be adding West Africa to our list of destinations next year because our daughter, husband, and three children are going as missionaries to Guinea, W. Africa, and we'll have to visit there to keep up with our grandchildren.

STORY EIGHTEEN

Alice Kohn and Family
Ileostomy, United States
"What to do When You Can't Stay Home"

On the morning of January 17, 1994 we were up early, showering and making last minute preparations for a trip to the hospital with our son, who was scheduled for a pull-through surgery. For those of you not living in Northridge, California, at the time, that date may not be forever etched in your memory. We were rocked by a major earthquake. We lived a mile from the now infamous Northridge Meadows, which collapsed. Our apartment, along with many others, was condemned. Once "red tagged" we were not even allowed to return until the building was deemed safe enough to enter.

In anticipation of the surgery, we had gotten lower than usual in our stock of supplies. We had about a day's worth of formula, diapers, and few ostomy supplies. We did have a pack of diapers, canned formula, and other supplies in an earthquake kit, only to have it rendered completely inaccessible. We were lucky to leave our apartment with anything. Socks that I had bought for the hospital were passed out to complete strangers; blankets were divided among neighbors who had come out in their pajamas. We grabbed what food and clothing we could, but were unable to make it to our earthquake kit, which had first aid supplies, ostomy supplies, food and clothing, and other necessities like a can opener, forks and water. We had dedicated the lower half of linen cabinets to emergency supplies and our earthquake supplies, but with all the shifting and collapse of the building, we couldn't get anything out.

Everything was overturned; it looked like someone had taken our apartment, picked it up, and shook it upside down.

Luckily the injuries our family sustained were minor, the most severe being my husband's shoulder, which was hurt trying to break down our Aunt's door. This John Wayne-type injury was one of those more common in the emergency room at this time. My husband was actually provided with a free lesson on how best to use the body safely to knock a door in.

Many grocery stores were closed for several days, and things like Pampers and formula were available at Red Cross disaster centers, but not special formulas, and certainly not ostomy supplies. We were fortunate to have relatives put us up on the floor for several days, until we found a new apartment. At the local Albertson's store, where we used to live, they were selling bare essentials— bread and water. A very nice employee actually scaled over collapsed shelves and overturned cases of broken food to get us our son's most needed special formula. In about a week, our HMO's pharmacy was able to replenish us with ostomy supplies. We actually ran out of ostomy supplies, and got creative with cloth diapers, washcloths, and ace bandages. You have to understand, our hospital was in another area code, and we couldn't even dial out of our area code. I wasn't able to call home to Oklahoma for a week.

There was no phone service in the house we were staying in, and the lines at the local pay phones were VERY long. It was an unusual, unforgettable experience.

We ended up moving down the block to a smaller apartment, but were happy to have a place, since they were in high demand. The surgery, of course, was rescheduled. It wasn't however, rescheduled late enough for me, as we had another powerful aftershock while he was hospitalized. I was in the hospital cafeteria at the time, and quickly returned to the pediatric unit, to find pictures askew, and many children crying.

Another tip, make sure someone else knows how to care for your beloved ostomate's needs. I had to pack, carry and clean, but still needed to watch my child, because I had never shown anyone else how to help him. Find someone who is willing to be on call for your family. Make sure that others know how to help your child, wife, or brother so that you are not the only person they have available in their hour of need. Keep complete instructions accessible, along with a medical history, and "make and model" of your ostomy supplies for the pharmacist. Let these instructions be your voice in your absence or inability to speak. Be the Boy Scout in the neighborhood—BE PREPARED. We now keep several days' worth of supplies in a backpack by the door, in my purse, in the diaper bag, and we always bring a fresh change into the car when we are leaving to go out somewhere. When we go to the hospital, we bring enough for a week, because, little did I know, they don't always have pediatric ostomy supplies readily available. I can tell you a 2 1/2-inch flange looks mighty large on those who happen to weigh in less than 40 pounds! The bags dangle between the knees! Both of our children now keep their beloved Barbie ™ and Elmo ™ backpacks ready with personal water bottles, change of clothing, extra diapers and wipes that are replaced regularly with a fresh supply, in addition to a coloring book, crayons, and a duplicate of their favorite toy. Our son's backpack has a large stock of ostomy supplies, his medical instructions, non-latex gloves, and an EPI PEN™ and Benadryl™ (due to latex allergy) packed inside as well. My backpack has a change of clothes, pictures, a copy of my address book, and my inhaler and full bottles of my current prescriptions. We still have an earthquake kit, and I hope it's more accessible than the first one was. It's also bigger, and better!

Keep lots of supplies accessible, in good amount, in addition to your prescription medication. It's even a good idea to have your doctor write out an extra prescription for ostomy supplies, to take with you in your luggage, just in case. I now know that *you just never know*! This may not seem to apply to travel, except that you don't know what might happen where you're going—or just when you'll be getting back.

STORY NINETEEN

Ingrid Johnson
Ileostomy, United States
"Adapting to Different Environments"

It takes a certain amount of knowledge and imagination to handle situations involving heat, cold, humidity, aridity, altitude and temperature. With a little bit of ingenuity, handling an ileostomy, colostomy or urostomy in any and all situations should allay any fears and insecurities about traveling or just living a normal, full life. A good case in point was a recent, strenuous geology field project I was involved in over a period of two weeks. At the time of the trip, I had had my ileostomy for about 3 1/2 months. I live in Arizona, and the trip entailed traveling via Colorado to the Southeast to a site near Elk Mountain at an elevation of 9,500 feet with no facilities except individual tents and a nearby stream for washing. We had to hike 12 to 16 miles every day with a full backpack in every type of weather, terrain and elevation extreme. I decided before leaving home to carry around three times the normal amount of ostomy supplies for the time span in case of problems or unavailability of supplies.

Since the surgery I had had some leak-age, skin irritation and short wear time prob-lems with my appliance. Also, my difficulties were compounded by a retracted stoma. I was able to find information on the Internet to help me find products and ways of applying them that worked.

On my way to Wyoming, I stopped at Sul-fur Hot Springs in Colorado. To my delight, the faceplate and pouch stayed put with no leakage as I experimented with hot spring pools ranging in temperature from 93° to 112° (Fahrenheit). I stayed in the hot water for about two hours total. To give my appliance a little extra protection, I covered every side of the faceplate with waterproof tape. Persons sensitive to waterproof tape could use non-allergenic tape first, then apply a layer of waterproof tape.

After a successful experiment at the hot springs, I decided to drive through some of the high country in the Rocky Mountains and continued up past Leadville at an elevation of approximately 11,000 feet. There was still ice on the lakes in June. I hiked around there for a while and was pleased to find that the cold had no effect on my appliance, even though I was wearing shorts. By the time I arrived at the field camp area I was feeling confident that I was not going to run into any major problems. I pitched a tent in a beautiful field of water irises and soon found out why they were growing there. I was in a swamp! By the time I discovered water was seeping through the bottom of the tent it was getting dark and was too late to move. I had to make the best of it. There were no facilities at the campsite, so I got very creative with Ziploc bags. I would empty the pouch into a baggie and then bury it—so I had less of a problem than the "squatters" did. I figured I really had the upper hand—*there are advantages to having an ostomy*! I also carried individually packaged sanitary wipes for cleaning up. Every night I'd go to the stream, scoop up water in a backpacking bottle and clean out my pouch in the bushes, well away from the stream.

I noticed no appreciable change in the pouch with changes in altitude. Some articles about ostomy appliances had mentioned "blowing up with air" as a result of increasing altitude but I think the small amount of air in my pouch was the result of geology camp food! To relieve the air build up I just popped the seal on the pouch once in a while. We did go through a lot of elevation changes during climbing and mapping and I also did a lot of bending and straining to get my work done. I found that a larger wafer works very well; it bends with the body and seems to stand up better to changes in temperature. For swimming, however, a smaller flange is more flexible and is easier to conceal under a swimsuit. I have been able to keep appliances on for seven or more days even though I swam every day. I also like to take hot baths every night and have had no problems keeping the face-plate on. Drying the faceplate with a hairdry-er as soon as you come out of the water helps to lengthen its life.

I recently attended a dog show in Washington state, which means rain, high humidity, bugs and porta-johns. Our campsite was quite far from the porta-john area, and during the night, I developed a leak. It was raining and there was no hope of getting into a dry situation. I grabbed a flashlight and headed for the nearest porta-john. It was very humid in the porta-john so I knew I would have a problem with adhesion. The only thing I could think of using to "dry" the area around my stoma was the baby powder I carry as an emergency deodorant. Before I attached the wafer I dusted the skin right under it and around it with the baby powder.

Pat Matranga,
Colostomy and Urostomy, United States
"Traveling with Two Ostomies"

I've had my colostomy for 23 years and my urostomy for five years. Bermuda is the furthest I've been from home (which is California). I only had my colostomy at that time and it was my first time on an airplane—not just with an ostomy—but my first time ever on an airplane. This was in 1987. I used the bathroom right away so I could see how much room I had to work with. They sure have small bathrooms on planes! Anyway, I had no problems until we were about three hours into our flight. I needed to empty my bag and did so. However, while I was still sitting on the toilet, a light came on that said for everyone to return to his or her seat. The light no sooner came on than we started experiencing turbulence. I kept trying to stand up and kept getting thrown back down on the toilet. It was not fun! This went on for about five minutes. I was a little afraid that a flight attendant would open the door to see if I was alright. I got out of there so fast as soon as the turbulence ended and after that every time I've been on an airplane, I DON'T take my time about emptying. Luckily, I was already finished emptying my bag when we hit the turbulence or I would have had a mess on my hands (literally). While in Bermuda, we stayed with our son and daughter-in-law who were stationed there. I had no accidents or awful experiences while there. I have had my urostomy since 1994 and since I've had both ostomies, I haven't done a whole lot of traveling. We had to move to Idaho for seven months because of my husband's job. We flew there to check things out for a week.

No problems on the flight or at the motel. We drove there when we moved and had both of our little dogs with us. We stopped at every rest area along the way for the dogs and me. One thing I do at all motels and whenever we stay anywhere away from home is to use a waterproof crib pad on the bed. As a matter of fact, I use one here at home too under the sheet. While away from home, I have never soiled the pad. At home I have from trying to go that one extra day before changing my appliances. When away from home, I change a day early just so I don't have to worry. I used a bedside drainage bag at night for the first two years I had my urostomy. Since I wake up several times a night to use the bathroom, I finally figured out that I didn't need to use the night bag (I'm a slow learner). I do have a suggestion for anyone with a urostomy who uses the bedside drainage bag and travels. I always took a few large drawstring kitchen garbage bags with me. I would put the night bag inside the garbage bag and tighten the drawstring, then hang the bag or if there was no place to hang it, I would lay it on the floor with no worry of any leaks. It did spring a leak one time while we were staying at a relative's house and I was so thankful it was inside that garbage bag. It also helps when you are staying at a relative or friend's house and have to walk down the hallway in the morning to use the bathroom. You can unhook from the night bag and leave it in the garbage bag until you have an opportunity to empty it rather than carrying it for everyone to see first thing in the morning. When traveling, I ALWAYS take about three or four times the amount of supplies I will need. I have never needed them but it sure helps knowing that I don't have to worry about that. I also take plenty of M9™ Drops with me and a good bathroom deodorizer. Usually with the M9™ Drops, there is no need for a deodorizer—I just like to be overly prepared. My carry-on bag for plane trips has all of my supplies, washrags, and at least two changes of clothes.

Traveling with two ostomies has caused me no more problems than traveling with one ostomy. I do try to make sure that I change my appliances on consecutive days rather than trying to change them both on one day. It saves time and makes things much easier.

STORY TWENTY-ONE

Chrystal Scotti
Ileostomy, United States
"Backpacking Adventures"

When I was asked to write this story on traveling with an ostomy, my first thought was, "What do I know about traveling with an ostomy? I just do it." Well, that's how I've lived my life since ostomy surgery: I've just done it. I was given back my life, given another chance to live. So that's what I've done, just lived it without having to worry about how to do it. So, from my experiences, I will attempt to address the issue of traveling with an ostomy.

Now, let's explore some of the modes of travel. Of course, everyone travels by car. And if you're going on a long trip, planning ahead is always advisable. Be sure to have plenty of supplies with you just in case. You never know what can happen. Be sure to take plenty of breaks to keep yourself comfortable.

Until recently, I had never traveled by plane, but I heard a lot of conflicting things about air travel. I wasn't sure what it was going to be like, but I do now; and since I only know what I experienced, I will only offer that here. When you do travel by air, be sure that you take your ostomy supplies with you in your carry-on baggage. Never be separated from your supplies. You never know when your luggage is going to get lost. As for the plane trip, I found it to be uneventful as far as the ostomy goes. Neither the pressure nor the altitude affected my ostomy at all. There are others who perhaps will have different experiences. Plan ahead and have plenty of supplies with you, just in case.

Some of the other modes of travel, of course, are bus and train. My family and I even traveled from the Lower 48 to Alaska by ferry. With all modes of public transportation that I've listed here, you will find that sometimes the facilities are a bit small for comfort. People who have ostomies have to adapt sometimes to the small, cramped facilities, but it can be done. If there are handicapped facilities available, I will use them only if they are not needed by others who are more needy than myself. This gives you a bit more room for comfort.

And don't ever let anyone make you feel guilty about using the handicapped stall in a public restroom. Just because you are not in a wheelchair doesn't mean that you don't need the facilities due to your handicap. Now, don't get me wrong, I'm the last person who would say that I'm handicapped, but technically speaking, we are, as we have had major surgery that has changed a vital function of our bodies. That's not to say we need to park in handicapped parking and start taking advantage of that sort of thing, but when available, and when doing so would not be taking the room away from others who may need it more than you, go ahead and use the facilities.

Another mode of travel, of course, is walking. I've not let anything associated with having an ostomy stop me from doing anything I want. Twelve years ago, when I became pregnant with my first child, my husband and I had planned a hiking/backpacking trip with some other couples. The day we left for our trip was the day we found out I was pregnant. I was only six weeks along.

When we got to the trailhead in the hills of Fillmore, California, where the backpacking trip was to start, the warning sign should have stopped me, but my need to prove that I could do it took over any common sense I (should have) had. The temperature out there that morning was 95 degrees, and it got up to 109 by midday. Between my husband and me, we only had about one gallon of water. That is not nearly enough liquid for anyone in that kind of heat for the length of time that we had planned, but we didn't want the extra weight.

Before we left, we were told by someone who "knew" the trail and had traversed it many times that it was a pretty easy hike into the camp we were heading to, and it was "flat" most of the way. So we figured we would just go ahead and hike to the camp and take it easy along the way. After all, there were supposedly springs of mountain water along the way that was safe for drinking. Well, this "easy" hike quickly turned into a very hard climb. We were going up long, steep hills, and down very short not-so-steep hills. There were very few flat places on the trail. Then when we got to the point where we were to head down into the campground, it was a treacherous, winding trail along the side of the mountain. By this time, it was midday, I was completely out of water, and we didn't see any springs along the trail. The heat, with the lack of water and the weight we were carrying, took its toll on me.

We got to that point on the trail, and I turned around and told my husband I was going home. Little did we know that that's where the "adventure" would begin. I turned around and went as far as I could go. Finally, I stopped, sat down in the trail and said, "I can't go any further. You have to go out and get help." He was so insistent that I go with him, more out of fear of leaving me there alone, but it was just impossible. By this time, I was getting severely dehydrated and having abdominal cramping. And being pregnant was another reason I had no business being out there, but I didn't want to spoil the fun. I love hiking and camping. This was just bad timing all the way around.

He set me up under a tree in the shade, with all my needs around me, and he literally ran out of there. What took us several hours of hiking took him about 30 to 60 minutes to run out. He ran down the hills and walked briskly up the inclines. Once he got off the trail, he found the park ranger. Because we were so far back into the back country, and the trail was a hiking trail only, the only way they could get help in was to fly the rescue helicopter in after me.

Before very long, I saw the helicopter flying above, so I came out from underneath the tree and was waving and hollering at the helicopter. A lot of good my hollering at the helicopter did! Anyhow, they landed about

300 yards away, and I thought, "Well, that's the only place they could land, and they are going to walk over here and get me," so I sat down and waited. Little did I know, another couple was hiking back out. The helicopter picked them up and left. I was shocked. I thought, "What are they doing? I'm right here." Again, all the hollering I was doing at the helicopter didn't help a bit.

They took that couple out and picked up my husband and came back for me. They hadn't even seen me the first time, but with my husband in the helicopter they found me right away. And they were only 300 yards away the first time! They had a doctor with them who checked me before transporting me. Then they loaded us and our gear into the helicopter, flew my husband to the trail-head so he could get our car, and then took me on to the hospital. I spent a few hours in the hospital, where they forced fluids into me and treated me for heat stroke and severe dehydration.

As for the helicopter ride, well, it was a very different experience. Nothing like flying in a plane. But don't go about taking a helicopter ride the way I did! I was embarrassed, but was able to laugh about it later. Just another adventure in what we call life.

So be prepared whenever you travel anywhere by any means. Make sure you have plenty of supplies with you just in case; make sure you have plenty of liquids, water, juice, or some type of electrolyte drink, especially if it is hot where you're going. Also, eat sensibly while traveling so as not to make your trip uncomfortable.

If you have had your ostomy for years, like me (I've had mine for over 15 years now), you know what you can and what you cannot eat, what your body will react adversely to. So, while traveling, stay on a sensible diet. And for those of you who have not had your ostomy for long, and are planning a trip, don't try anything new to eat. You don't want to be uncomfortable and have any severe problems, as you won't have all the comforts of home where you're going. And most of all, use common sense when you go anywhere.

STORY TWENTY-TWO

Tom Sowerbutt,
Ileostomy, United States
"Traveling in Russia"

I have had an ileostomy since 1980 and have had my share of problems with it. I have had to have several further operations after the original and in 1997 had to have the full surgery yet again. It was a success and to celebrate my wife and I decided to treat ourselves. After looking through several tour brochures we were intrigued by the idea of visiting Russia by coach—which would of course have a toilet. After receiving many reassurances from the tour company regarding my ileostomy we booked our tickets and waited in anticipation.

We were picked up not too far from our home and despite having to change the coach on a number of occasions all was going well. Then just as we were about to leave the UK the tour guide gave us all a briefing about the trip.

During the briefing we were left with no illusions and were assured that we were in for a few surprises in the East—not the least of which was the lack of toilet facilities. The tour guide advised that there were no toilet stops en route to our destinations and we wouldn't be able to use the onboard toilet as he would have difficulties finding anywhere in the East to empty it. My wife and I were shocked to say the least. I wondered what we had gotten ourselves into. So I had a talk with the guide and showed him a card I carry which basically says that I have a medical condition and require access to facilities. He assured me that there would be no problems and that under the circumstances I should use the toilet if necessary.

My only problem then was that I didn't want the other passengers to know I had an ileostomy. Being the only person on board being allowed to visit the toilet en route I felt would have given the game away. We had a great holiday but it was a strain. I had to cut back on my food so that I didn't need to visit the onboard toilet. It is a long way to Russia on a coach from the UK and I had to sometimes wait several hours before I could use a hotel toilet at our daily destinations. In between we had what the guide called bush stops—that's right, bush stops. The coach pulled up in a lay-by near woods and men went one way and the women another to relieve themselves. On a number of occasions when toilets were available at lunchtime they were inadequate and once a shared toilet was no more than a couple of squats with a two-foot barrier separating men from women. Of course I carried toilet paper with me and believe me I needed to, as it usually wasn't provided except in hotels.

As I say we had a great holiday and nobody ever realized—I think—about my ileostomy. The tour guide appeared to try his hardest and I did notice some decent stops en route. But they had to keep to a schedule. I don't know what I would have done if I had had a dysfunction en route though. We traveled through France, Germany, Belarus, Russia, Finland, Sweden and back through Germany and France. I learned from my experience and now know that I can manage any journey to anywhere on the globe. I made new friends and it was a great experience for me. In fact I think I got much more out of the trip than anyone else on board that coach.

STORY TWENTY-THREE

Ron Titlebaum
J-Pouch, United States
"Traveling with a J-Pouch"

People with ostomies, throughout their lives, typically develop a backlog of unusual and interesting experiences. It is, after all, a strange plumbing arrangement requiring training and skill to master the fundamentals. Until you master the change and maintenance procedures, the unexpected should be expected. Without a sense of humor, you might as well stay home. With one—laugh and the world laughs with you, but maybe not exactly at the same time. I no longer have an ostomy. My procedure (alternative waste management hardware) is technically called an ileoanal anastomosis. There are many other names for it like the pelvic pouch, pull-through, or J or S pouch depending on its shape. It is quickly emerging, for those who qualify for it, as the main surgical alternative to an ileostomy. If you have ulcerative colitis or familial polyposis, require surgery and are in reasonably healthy condition otherwise, you're likely a candidate. With a J-pouch, your colon and rectum are both completely removed as they are in an ileostomy. However, the anal sphincter muscles are preserved. The surgeon uses the last 10 inches or so of your small intestine, the terminal ileum, to form a pouch or reservoir, about the size of a fist.

An opening at the base of the pouch is then attached to the inside of the anus. The pouch then functions like a mini-colon or rectum, both storing stool and absorbing water.

With a J-pouch, you use your anal sphincters for control and you go to the bathroom in the normal manner. The difference is that the J-pouch only does a percentage of the work previously done by the colon and rectum. You do get more water in the stool, so you need to empty it more often. The typical person with a J-pouch goes five or six times a day and one or two times at night. J-pouch stool is typically the consistency of toothpaste, but it doesn't take much to liquefy it still further. Dietary derelicts, like myself, go more often—depending upon the dietary abuse we heap upon ourselves. The other major concern is that the output from the ileum, pouch and anus is quite alkaline. A little stool on the skin around the anus causes perianal itching or burning, sort of the adult version of diaper rash. With looser stool, even with a Charles Atlas trained set of sphincters, leakage can be a potential problem for certain people with this procedure.

So the travel issues for those with a J-pouch surround the characteristics and outcome of the plumbing: a smaller stool reservoir means more frequent BMs; more liquid stool mean the sphincters must work harder—and be ever vigilant; and leakage, if it occurs, can feel like sitting in a puddle of sulfuric acid. This is the trade some J-pouchers make not to wear an ostomy appliance. It's critical to add that doing the right dietary things ameliorates these conditions more than anything else does. There's a pretty good list of dos and don'ts. But a little abuse goes a long way. And speaking frankly, it's these abuses that make life a little more fun.

Most often it takes two operations to complete the J-Pouch procedure. In stage one, the doctor removes the colon and rectum, makes the internal pouch, but leaves the patient with an ileostomy. This allows the pouch and anastomosis to heal before it is used. In the second operation, the ileostomy is removed and the pouch goes into service. My favorite travel story occurred during the in-between stage for me.

I was flying from Boston to Orange County, California. On this particular trip I decided to go through St. Louis. About a half-hour before we were scheduled to land in St. Louis, I noticed a small, dark stain on my fortunately dark trousers. One of the first things you learn at a UOA support group meeting is never pack your ostomy supplies in your suitcase. Always use your carry-on for this. At least I had the good sense to do this.

With the "Return to Seat" light on in the latrine of a Boeing 737 due to landing momentarily, there's neither time nor space for an appliance change. So I improvised as much as possible, packing about a half roll of toilet paper for absorption into my pants and taping it down as best I could. This bought me enough time and absorbency to get to the bathroom in the terminal. It was about noon and the terminal was getting busy. It turned out that this particular men's room had only one stall and two urinals. I got lucky and the stall was empty. I set about to change my appliance in a space with no horizontal surfaces except the floor, the toilet itself and the ever so small cover of the toilet paper dispenser. I won't go into the details, but to change an appliance involves removing your trousers and underpants, removing the appliance, cleaning the stoma area, mounting the new appliance, and then getting dressed again. On top of this is the disposal problem of the old and, shall we say, slightly soiled appliance. To do this in a toilet stall configured as above, requires exactly eight leg lifts, 14 right turns, 14 left turns and 12 complete rotations. At best, in this circumstance, one can do this in nine minutes. I took twelve. Unbeknownst to me, the line waiting for the stall was growing rapidly. Everybody in line, with their own needs and pressures, could see my feet and the bottom 12 inches of my legs. At last I finished and opened the door. I walked out whistling Blue Skies. Nobody in the crowd said anything! But if looks could kill, I wouldn't be here today. What do you think they thought I was doing? "Smile and the world smiles with you, but only if they don't kill you first!"

I've also had some interesting moments with my J-pouch. Most of them seem to involve drinking and traveling. A fairly common medical problem for some J-pouchers is an inflammation of the pouch lining called "pouchitis." The drug of choice for this condition is an antibiotic called Flagyl ™. Flagyl comes with a warning not to consume alcohol while using this drug. It can cause upset stomach and nausea. I had been on and off Flagyl and knew that I could tolerate wine or beer in small quantities with no consequence. On this one trip, since I was traveling business class and the booze was free, I decided to try a Canadian Club™, about three quarters of an hour before landing. Nothing at all happened until the plane landed, taxied to the gate and the people started to stand in the aisles to disembark. Good grief—it hit like tidal wave. My stomach and pouch simultaneously said "Empty me right now you stupid bozo!" I couldn't go forward or backward for what seemed like 10 minutes. I somehow willed my body into submission until I got off the plane and found a bathroom. I decided to go head first, feeling it was the more urgent of the urges. It was only for seconds, but I bet against another unfortunate J-pouch phenomenon, "scrambled brownies." The decision cost me another pair of underpants. I never did that again.

Another time, I was in Japan, on business and we had had a sensational dinner with customers, about 50 miles from our hotel in Tokyo. As I said, I love my beverages. Indeed it's known that ileostomates and J-pouchers should consume more fluids to compensate for the loss that goes out in our more liquid stool. I have always taken this responsibility seriously. But obviously, when in Rome . . .

In this case the liquid was a combination of Japanese beer and hot sake, not mixed but properly consumed in tandem. This in itself should not be problematic when reasonable restraints are applied. But it turns out that "reasonable" is a major variable. What's reasonable in your hotel may not be reasonable when facing a one-hour commute on the Japanese Railway. The good news is that there are toilets on the Japanese trains (not the subways). The bad news is that the toilets are the eastern, squat-and-pray style. This, by itself, is difficult enough for westerners, but adding the handicaps of a moving train, a confined space, no handgrips and an inability to focus correctly renders normal function virtually impossible. Well anyhow, there goes another clean pair! Can you see why you need a sense of humor?

One time I was on a Caribbean cruise that stopped in Caracas, Venezuela. We had the choice of the city tour or the much more rugged, unpredictable jungle tour. My wife went to town. I went with the loonies. At 8 a.m., they loaded us on oversized four-wheel drive vehicles, each with six people and two case of the local brew. It was a sacrifice but somebody had to do it! Hi ho, hi ho, to the jungle we did go. By 10:00 a.m., while climbing up a back country waterfall to enjoy the slide down, the local brew worked its magic. Oh no, not again. Okay, here's the scene: the native flora provides the cover, but the jungle is dense, and in the foliage could be any poison-spreading species of insect. It certainly wasn't the maple or oak leaves I've come to cherish. Oh well, what's one more pair!

With most alternative plumbing arrangements, performance of your lower GI system is generally more "fragile." In my case I live the line from the old TV show, Beretta: "Don't do the crime, if you can't do the time." If you really want to enjoy freedom from intestinal stress, pay very close attention to the dietary rules. If not, be flexible. And have plenty of pairs of underpants!

STORY TWENTY-FOUR

"Gregory"[4]
Ileostomy, United States
"Outdoor Adventures"

My name is Gregory and I'm an ostomate. In fact, I'm the only one of my kind in the

[4] Excerpt is reprinted with permission from the *Ostomy Quarterly*, Volume 33, Number 6, November 1996, "From Sea to Sky."

world. I'm the only ostomate who is currently a certified scuba instructor, and an FAA licensed commercial pilot, and certified flight instructor. As ostomates, we are unique and surely different from non-ostomates. Still, we are no less able to attain our dreams and goals. Our plumbing differs from that of others, and that's it. Otherwise, ostomates are no different from anyone else.

It's a hard thing to do, to try to summarize your life in a few short pages, but I write my story with one purpose: to show other ostomates, first hand, that we are more than capable of leading perfectly normal lives, if we choose. And that life can be as, if not more, fulfilling than ever before. After a two-year struggle, I came to the realization that I needed to control my life, and that I am no longer controlled by my ostomy. What a great feeling!

Since my ostomy surgery, a lot has happened. I've taught scuba diving, as well as flying. I've been snow skiing, water skiing, and sailing. I still ride my bicycle, and I love to shoot my 9 mm SigSauer at the gun club. I even tried skydiving from 12,500 feet. Four months after ostomy surgery, I went skiing in Snowbird, Utah. There, I found some of the steepest and most challenging skiing I've ever encountered. When I ski, there's no holding back. Mostly, I ski the steep, fast, expert trails. One day while attempting a jump, I caught some big air and wiped out.

Needless to say, my pouch broke. So I went into an area full of trees, and put on a new one. That was that, and off I went. I absolutely refuse to let my ostomy make a conservative skier out of me. I'll never ski slowly or cautiously for fear that my pouch will burst. If it does, I'll clean up and move on.

Scuba diving is another story. In 120 feet of water the pressure exerted on our bodies is five times greater than that on land and our air cavities (sinuses, lungs, intestines, etc.) are affected the most. In theory, intestinal surgery could pose a problem. While Scuba diving, we breathe compressed air. Nitrogen bubbles form in our body tissues, and they must be expelled prior to surfacing. If not, one could experience decompression sickness. To avoid this all divers utilize "tables." These are scientifically based guidelines explaining how long a human may breathe compressed air at a specific depth without getting "the bends."

Dive tables were originally designed by the US Navy, and greatly modified over the last 50 years. Today, many divers use underwater computers to do this for them. I use a combination of the two. Still, however, I'm a conservative diver. Maybe even more so since my surgery. I'll still go deep, but I won't push the limits. According to the dive tables, one can descend to 120 feet and remain there for 14 minutes. Given the same scenario, I'll only stay for 10 minutes.

I've made 75 dives, 22 of which were deeper than 100 feet since my surgery, and I've never had a problem. Before every dive, I empty my pouch, and that's it. My only suggestion is to dive slightly on the conservative side, and consult your surgeon. In order to learn to dive, you need a doctor's approval. Once approved, you're allowed to start training. Save yourself a lot of grief and consult your surgeon, not your Gastroenterologist.

As a Scuba instructor, many people ask me what drugs they are allowed to take while breathing compressed air. As always, my answer is "I'm not a medical doctor, I'm a scuba instructor." I remind these people to consult with their primary physicians to get a proper answer. As for me, however, I use a specific rule of thumb. If I need to take a drug, I'll start it several days before diving. Therefore, any side effects will be encountered on land. Imagine the tragedy if a drug's adverse reaction happened to a diver underwater. What if the drug made you very sleepy, or impaired your judgment; it could be fatal underwater. Even if it's only over-the-counter medication, this is still a good rule to follow.

In summation, my Crohn's and ostomy have made life really miserable at times. But the facts are the facts: I have a chronic disease, and it's not always going to be pleasant and pain free. Regardless, I'm just as active, if not more so, than ever before. My advice to ostomates is to seek out as much support as you can, and keep a positive mental attitude. Our only limitations are the ones our minds dictate.

Barbara Kupfer
Ileostomy, United States
"Traveling to Israel with a Pouch"

At the age of five it was discovered that I had ulcerative colitis. The case was mild and the few symptoms I had did not bother me. Once a year I would experience a flare up. In my 40s, the drug Sulphaziadine was prescribed and at age 54 I was diagnosed with colon cancer. On June 1, 1997, my colon was removed and I had an ileostomy. The cancer did not spread; hence I did not need chemotherapy or radiation. An agreement was made with the pouch at that time. It had to adjust to my lifestyle rather than the reverse.

My husband and I planned to be in Israel for two weeks. I have packed my bags a few times, the destination being Israel. Why was December 1998 going to be different? How many supplies shall I pack is a question I never asked myself. When not traveling, I change my little pouch every 7 to 10 days. I decided to more than double the amount I would usually use, along with extra paste, powder and tape. When away from home I think you feel more secure knowing you have enough supplies, just in case.

Israel is a country of immense richness and diversity, both in its natural setting and the remains of the past. Its length can be driven in less than eight hours and the climate and topography varies greatly from north to south. Its diversity is nowhere better reflected than in its people: Lithuanians, Moroccans, Yemenites, Poles, Germans, Turks, Russians, Americans, and Ethiopians are among the Jewish communities of modern Israel. It is home to three of the world's great religions, Christianity, Judaism and Islam. Together with the country's non-Jewish citizens—Muslim and Christian, Arab, Bedouin and Druze—the melting pot gives the country its exceptional flavor.

The plane trip from Boston to Tel Aviv is 12 hours. It is a good idea to drink plenty of fluids while on a plane for that long. Special meals can be ordered 24 hours prior to boarding. I ordered an Indian dinner that was very good. Emptying my pouch on the plane was easy using my water bottle. Once in Israel my husband and I traveled through Tel Aviv, Jerusalem, Eilat and other interesting cities. We went for long walks, ate in excellent restaurants and sampled falafel and hummus along with other Middle Eastern specialties. The food agreed with my little pouch most of the time. Since the climate was dry, I always carried a bottle of drinking

water along with a bottle of water to empty
my pouch.

On this trip I had three problems of different severity. The first two were minor leaks,
but the third was a leak and spillage from the
wafer. Let me elaborate on the third.

We went to Haifa on December 31, in
the mid-morning in order to be back to Tel
Aviv by evening to celebrate New Year's Eve
at a hotel party. Haifa is Israel's third largest
city, the country's main port and an industri-
al center. It is set on the wooded slopes of
Mount Carmel overlooking the Mediterranean Sea. The day was sunny and cool and
the drive was a pleasant hour and a half. We
had lunch with friends and were able to
spend the afternoon with them. Before leaving Haifa, I emptied my pouch for the trip
back to Tel Aviv. Once on the road, a heavy
storm greeted us. Traffic came to a halt on
the highway. We were not moving. Men were
leaving their cars to visit the brush off the
road. I felt an explosion coming out of the
wafer and could not even check it. After a few
hours, traffic started to move slowly, but there
were no bathrooms or places to stop. Finally
a sign for a town called Hadera. We exited
the highway and went into town, where I
found a Burger King™ with a clean bathroom. It was the many carrots I had for lunch
that caused the problem. I cleaned the mess
and decided to change the appliance when I
reached Tel Aviv, an hour away. December

31, 1998 was coming to an end and I had a new pouch for the New Year but we missed the New Year's Eve Party at the hotel.

There was not an occasion that the pouch prevented me from enjoying the many things to do and see in Israel. I feel that I am in control of my pouch.

CHAPTER THREE

Wheelchairs and Ostomies

Mary Jane Wolfe

As a woman who was born with spina bifida, I have a neurogenic bladder and partial paralysis in my lower extremities. Although I can use crutches, I find myself using my wheelchair almost exclusively now because the wheelchair allows me to get from one place to another more quickly and with less energy exerted than if I had relied on my crutches. I did not have ostomy surgery until I was 17 and believe me that traveling with a urostomy is a lot more pleasant than traveling with diapers. When I went to camp for a week in my early teens, I had to have at least one large suitcase with extra bedding for nighttime and I spent a lot of time washing the bedding and my diapers since this was before the age of disposable diapers. Now when I travel for long periods of time, I only have to carry a few ostomy pouches, barriers or wafers, and a night drainage system.

I am a managing editor for a major textbook publisher with three offices in Massachusetts, New Jersey, and Illinois and I am an active volunteer. I travel often for business trips, conferences, meetings, or other events associated with my volunteer activities, and an occasional vacation. I have never let my ostomy or my wheelchair stop me from going anywhere and I am sure my friends and relatives would confirm this statement. Here are a few of my travel experiences along with some tips and advice.

I drive my own two-door car with the use of hand controls. I sit in the driver's seat and then pull the wheelchair directly behind me in the back seat. One advantage to driving myself is that I can decide when I want or need to stop for a "potty" or rest stop. I prefer to stop at local fast food restaurants because they almost always have a wheelchair accessible bathroom unlike most gas stations. When I was traveling with my parents and my father was driving, my mother would often motion to me that she needed to stop to go to the bathroom. You see my dad would stop if I said I had to go to the bathroom but would not necessarily stop if my mother made the request! When I travel with others, I have realized that I do not need to stop any more often than my traveling companions.

When I was in college, I experienced dealing with a "community" bathroom although at least about 30 years ago, the bathrooms were not coed. I soon learned that if I was planning to change my appliance, I needed to get organized enough so that I would not be in the middle of a change and realize I had left an important item in my dorm room. I changed my appliance in a bathroom stall so I attempted to do this at odd times when others were not in a hurry to use the stall too.

I have always loved to swim so I often find myself in YMCA locker rooms where women are changing clothes out in the open. I could change in and out of my swimsuit in a bathroom stall, but I find these to be rather confining so I usually do as others are doing. I usually drape my towel across the middle of my body to hide the ostomy and many of my scars when I am moving from the shower area to the dressing area. Then depending on what I am dressing into, I leave my towel wrapped around my body and either dress the top or bottom half of me first. When I finally remove the towel, there is only a small part or no part of my opaque pouch showing. Some women prefer to wear pouch covers at times and I tried these for a while but putting the pouch cover on or off before and after swimming or showering seemed to be more conspicuous to me. Of course the key to dressing after swimming or showering is always toweling off the area around your pouch adequately.

I am not a big camper but when I was in college I was a camp counselor and several times during that summer I camped out overnight. My favorite camping experience was sleeping in a sleeping bag next to a lake and falling asleep to the waves hitting the seashore in a regular pattern. Other times we would take some kids on a canoe trip and sleep in a sleeping bag near an open fire. In both situations I considered whether to carry my night drainage system and then have to worry about emptying and cleaning it in the morning. I decided that since the excursions were only one night that I should not bother with the night drainage. Instead I would roll out of my sleeping bag when my pouch got full and crawl around on my fanny away from the sleeping area until I could dig a small hole in the sand or dirt, empty my pouch into the hole, and then cover the hole before crawling back to my sleeping bag. It may not have been the most sanitary method of emptying my pouch but I did not want to miss these experiences and as long as I made sure no one was watching me I felt it was a good method of "roughing it." However I definitely prefer vacations involving hotel stays rather than sleeping bags.

Now I am going to tell you about some of my plane adventures. I have flown all over the continental United States and to Hawaii,

Canada, Peru, and England. I would like to travel more overseas but it is money and time off work that has prevented this so far—not my wheelchair or ostomy.

First of all here is some advice. If you are flying and have your own wheelchair, check any baggage, and then be prepared to be "frisked," or hand checked, if you are unable to walk through the security door. If you have an ostomy, it is a good idea to try and empty your pouch before going through security. The staff members have to check everyone very closely now so if you do have a full pouch, you might have to explain the bulge. I have had security guards even ask me about the hump on my back because they have to be certain you are not trying to hide something. Good guards will even ask you to lift your body so that they can check your seat cushion and also check under your wheelchair. After this, you need to check in at the gate even if you checked your bags. At the gate you should remind the personnel that you need a "gate tag" or "escort tag" for your wheelchair. If you forget to remind the airline staff and the person is unacquainted with this system, your wheelchair may be sent to the baggage area when you arrive at your destination—rather than at the gate so that you can wheel yourself to the baggage area. If you cannot walk to your seat on the plane, you should also ask for an "aisle chair." You transfer from your wheelchair to this narrow

aisle chair and airline personnel then push
you and the aisle chair to your seat. To avoid
possibly delaying the whole flight, you should
attempt to be at the gate at least 30 minutes
before departure time for a US flight and at
least 60 minutes before an overseas flight.
Although I do not need to use an aisle chair,
I ask when the flight will pre-board and then
I make sure that I go to the bathroom about
10 minutes before the pre-boarding time.

If you normally do not use a wheelchair
but may have difficulty walking the long dis-
tances between the check-in area and the
gate, just ask for a wheelchair when you
check your bags. Someone will bring a wheelchair and push you to the gate area. Don't be
afraid to ask the person to stop at a restroom
on the way to the gate. These people do not
get paid very much so tips are appreciated.
When you arrive at your destination, there
should be another wheelchair and assistant
available but you may have to wait a few minutes. One time a little old lady saw my personal wheelchair while I was waiting on the
plane for everyone to debark. She sat in it
and had someone push her to the baggage
area until the airline personnel noticed the
mistake and retrieved my chair in exchange
for their wheelchair.

If you have an ostomy and cannot walk
to the bathroom on the plane, you need to
think about alternative solutions before taking the trip. First of all if the flight is short

and you empty your pouch prior to boarding the plane, there should be no problem. I happened to be experimenting wearing a pouch liner on one trip and when there was a longer delay than usual to land, the liner prevented a leakage. However if the flight time plus the early boarding time and debarking time is longer than the time you usually allow between emptying your pouch, you may need to consider a different routine. Some disabled people will wear slacks when traveling and connect the ostomy pouch to a leg bag worn on your calf. This allows at least twice as much time before the pouch via the leg bag would need to be emptied. This would probably be suitable for a transcontinental flight but may not work for a transatlantic or transpacific flight. Another possibility would be to connect your ostomy pouch or your leg bag to a night drainage system placed in a bag on the floor next to you covered by a blanket. Another option is to call before making reservations to ask if you could use the aisle chair during the flight to get to the bathroom. I have also seen grown men crawl to the bathroom if there was no other option but you also must consider the limited space in the airplane bathroom and determine if you could empty your pouch from the floor or need to lift yourself up to the toilet seat first. Where there is a will, there is a way—although it may not be the most convenient or conventional method.

Airlines have gotten better during the 30 years I have flown but some airline personnel still need to learn how to deal with disabled people as regular customers. One time I was flying from Chicago to Atlanta to visit my brother and his family for a week. I was waiting in line to check my suitcase when an airline employee insisted I get out of the line I was in because the airline had a line for "special situations" and I fit that category in his opinion. Reluctantly I left the line I was in and proceeded to get in the "special situations" line behind a couple with skis who I would find out later was going to Minneapolis. Unfortunately the night before I packed in a hurry and threw everything into the suitcase including my ostomy supplies, my eyeglasses, and my medicine. I forgot the cardinal rule about carrying your ostomy supplies and medicine with you. Anyway, the person checked my bag but when I arrived in Atlanta the bag was not there. I did not start to panic until 24 hours had gone by and I desperately needed the anti-diarrheal medicine that I take twice a day. I called my pharmacy in Chicago but the anti-diarrheal medicine was a controlled substance so the Federal government would not allow the pharmacy or my doctor to telephone a refill for me. My only resort was to get an appointment with a local doctor who would write me a prescription for the medicine. Even the ostomy supplies were more expensive because I could not use my insurance to cover 80 percent of the expense. Later that week I happened to be out on my brother's deck with my nieces and nephews when one of my contacts got dirt in it. The next thing I knew the contact disappeared under the deck and despite my efforts to retrieve it, I was left with one contact and fuzzy eyesight. Since I have poor eyesight, my parents even had to pick me up from the airport because I could not drive with only one good eye. I arrived home and filled out forms for the airline to reimburse me for the items in my suitcase. Would you believe that a week after I returned home (and two weeks after that airline employee insisted I change lines to get better treatment), my suitcase was found at the Minneapolis airport! The person who checked my bag thought that of course I was not traveling alone but must be traveling with the skiers that were in front on me in the "special situations" line. I guess the airline had planned a special situation just for me!

Another one of my favorite travel stories involved a trip to Hawaii. I was traveling with a girlfriend to visit a couple we knew who had moved to the main island of Hawaii. We did not want to impose so my girlfriend and I had decided to stay in a hotel the first night and then decide whether to stay with our friends or stay in the hotel the rest of the week. We spent the first night at our friends' house and before leaving for the hotel, I asked to use their bathroom. My friend pointed to an area in their back yard that was up a couple steps. I saw a toilet seat in the middle of the back yard surrounded by trees but definitely in the open. I used the excuse that I was too tired to walk up the steps and that I could wait until we got back to the hotel. That night my girlfriend and I debated whether to continue our hotel stay or stay with our friends. The main drawback to staying at the hotel was that our friends had to drive quite a distance on curvy roads each morning and night and we thought the drive each night was more of an imposition than staying with them. The main drawback to staying with our friends was the outdoor bathroom in the open but my girlfriend said if it did not bother me with my ostomy she could handle it too. The next day we told our friends we would stay with them but asked them how they handled the outdoor plumbing. Our friends laughed and told us that the toilet I saw was just an old toilet they were throwing out. They actually had an enclosed bathroom with a shower and private toilet that was hidden by the trees. Therefore we really did not have to "rough it" after all.

Everyone with an ostomy probably has their favorite story involving kids. I have two favorite stories that involve two of my nieces. One night I was helping my mother babysit my young niece who was about five years old at the time. The three of us were having a sleepover and were getting ready for bed at the same time. My mother, who had a prosthesis for one breast that had been removed because of cancer, did not even think about it until my niece asked her what it was. I laughed as my mother attempted to explain it to her. Then a few minutes later the roles were reversed. As I got out my night drainage system, my niece asked what that was. It was my mother's turn to laugh as I tried to explain my ostomy. We thought my niece would surely become a doctor or a nurse after her early education to breast prostheses and ostomy pouches.

The second story involved a different niece who happened to be about three years old when I came to visit her family. The first day she was my shadow. I could not go anywhere without her including the bathroom although I tried and finally gave up. I showed her how I went to the bathroom and at least that was the last time she followed me into the bathroom. A week went by and she never said anything about my explanation until she and my brother took me to the airport. Before I said goodbye to them, I told my brother that I had better go to the bathroom before boarding the plane. As I was wheeling down the hall to the bathroom I could hear my niece say in a rather loud voice, "Daddy, did you know that Aunt Janie goes pee pee in a bag!" My poor brother's face turned beet red!

As I hope you have learned by now, my travel stories are no different from those of other ostomates. Actually my wheelchair and ostomy have allowed me to travel to places I would never have dreamed of as a child when I could not even have a friend spend the night because of my diapers and the odor. Now I can even "sleep over with a member of the opposite sex" although this may be the subject for another book so I better quit!

CHAPTER FOUR

Don't Leave Home Without It!

What to take with you when you travel

Gwen B. Turnbull, RN, BS, CETN

'Tickets, please!' said the Guard, putting his head in at the window. In a moment everybody was holding out a ticket. 'Now then! Show your ticket, child!" the Guard went on, looking angrily at Alice... 'I'm afraid I haven't got one,' Alice said in a frightened tone: 'there wasn't a ticket office where I came from.' 'Don't make excuses,' said the Guard: 'you should have bought one from the engine-driver.' All this time the Guard was looking at her, first through a telescope, then through a microscope, and then through an opera glass. At last he said, 'You're traveling the wrong way,' and shut up the window and went away. [5]

It's easy to end up "traveling the wrong way" like Alice did in her adventures in Won-

---

[5] Lewis Carroll, *Alice's Adventures in Wonderland and Through the Looking Glass* (New York: Alfred A. Knopf, Everyman's Library Children's Classics, 1992).

derland and it can be disastrous. Regardless of your final destination—whether it's Wonderland, Wally World, Disneyland, Newfoundland, or Iceland—there are a few *travel essentials* that must be placed in your travel bag before you pack anything else.

- ✔ A spirit of adventure
- ✔ An open mind
- ✔ Flexibility
- ✔ A sense of humor
- ✔ Student's eyes

Life is an adventure. It's exciting because there's always something new to learn—to see for the first time, with "student's eyes." Through your experience with ostomy surgery, you've discovered how quickly life can throw a curve ball in your direction. A curve ball that literally turns your world upside down. Because of this experience, you've been forced to become more open-minded and adapt to new situations. You've learned to be flexible—to "go with the flow," so to speak. In effect, you've learned to "set a place at life's table for the unexpected guest." You've had experiences you thought would happen to someone else, but never you. You've had to learn new information quickly, new ways of doing things—and learned to laugh when things didn't go quite right. Believe it or not, these are the same qualities needed by the savvy and happy traveler.

You see? Your ostomy surgery has already packed those travel essentials in your suitcase for you! It's prepared you well to travel through the adventure we call Life—and therefore, has prepared you to travel wherever on this planet you choose to go in whatever way you choose to get there—train, plane, bicycle, car, llama, or on foot. If you didn't already have those five travel essentials in your travel bag, you simply wouldn't be reading a book on how to travel with an ostomy, now would you?

Quantity of Life versus Quality of Life

Frances Mayes, in her beautifully written best-selling book about her life in Italy, writes: "Change—the transforming experience—is part of the quest in traveling. Travel can reinforce the primitive urge to bring the new into the circle of the known."[6] People with ostomies have already had a transforming experience—the experience of creating an entirely new way of managing one of the most personal of human body functions. They've learned what it means to recover from the "ashes" of disease and to transform into a slightly different, but healthier person than they were before their surgery. Ostomy surgery added quantity to your life. Now, it's up to you to put the quality back into your life.

[6] Frances Mayes, *Bella Tuscany: The Sweet Life in Italy* (New York: Broadway Books, a division of Random House, Inc., 1999).

A Lesson from the Gridiron

In his book, *Alive & Kicking*,[7] Rolf Benirschke, the former place kicker for the San Diego Chargers, shares his reactions to his first lesson in self-care of his ileostomy and the impact it would have on the future of his life.

"I still wasn't convinced that I could lead a normal life. 'I don't know, Melba (his ET Nurse). I'm not sure I can handle all of this,' I blithely said. 'It's not a question of whether or not you can handle it,' she stated firmly. 'There's simply no option. Besides, if it weren't for the surgery, you'd be six feet under right now, and you wouldn't have any choice at all.' I stared at her. She had my attention now. 'Look, Rolf,' she said, as if she were reading my mind. 'These appliances are not going away, and you must learn how they work. For the rest of your life, you're going to have to do this. If you learn well, they shouldn't interfere with anything you do.'"

And so, when it comes to traveling, the biggest thing someone with an ostomy has to do is simply a little extra planning.

"Tell them to take the same things they would take on any trip."

In an effort to do a little research in preparation for writing this chapter, I wrote several of my colleagues asking what recommendations they made to their patients about what to take on a trip. One very wise ET Nurse wrote, "Tell them to take the same things they

[7] Rolf Benirschke, *Alive & Kicking* (San Diego: The Firefly Press, 1996).

would take on any trip." At first, I thought this was a bit dismissive. But after thinking about it and having spent many years of my own life traveling around the world, I thought that this was excellent advice and should be included in the chapter on what to bring. So here we go with first things first.

Imagine carrying your suitcase for several blocks by yourself.

The first rule in packing a suitcase is to imagine carrying it for several blocks by yourself. Luggage porters or hotel transfers from train stations and airports are not always available. Try to take only one suitcase, preferably one with wheels—avoiding bulky garment bags that can be difficult to carry.

I learned this lesson the hard way. On my first professional business trip abroad by myself, I vividly remember lugging two enormous and heavy suitcases up ancient bricked hilly roads in 90 degree heat—from the train station—to my hotel—in France—in the rain. I wasn't sure if dialing 911 in France would elicit the help I thought I would soon need! Today, I travel with one suitcase only. One with wheels.

Go Lightly

Try to keep your suitcase as lightweight was possible. Not only it is easier and more comfortable to carry a lighter suitcase, but people with ostomies shouldn't be lifting much more than 25 pounds due to the possibility of developing a peristomal hernia.

Transfer the contents of containers of cosmetics and shampoos and liquid ostomy accessories (such as deodorizers and skin powders and cleansers) into smaller plastic bottles and containers to lighten the load. Ask your medical supplier for sample sizes of the ostomy products you need. Remember that most hotels today provide various toiletries and appliances such as irons and hair dryers, at no charge, so it may not be necessary to lug those along. Pack a small collapsible umbrella or plastic poncho if your destination is a rainy one. Whatever you do, don't overstuff your suitcase. Leave room for souvenirs and other purchases you make. Better yet, throw in an empty collapsible nylon bag just in case you run out of room on the return trip.

Dress for Success

Your wardrobe can make or break your trip. Pack clothes that don't need ironing, that you can 'wash and wear' in your hotel room, and that mix and match. Select items that can be dressed up or down with the addition or removal of a jacket, tie, scarf, or jewelry. Take patterned or dark clothing that won't readily show wrinkles or the unfortunate results of a pouch leakage. Check out the weather at your destination and choose your clothes accordingly. Don't forget to take a jacket or sweater for use in air-conditioned rooms and stores.

Take lots of extra socks, stockings, and underwear. Don't take more than one or two pairs of shoes, and make sure the ones you do take can be mixed and matched with the clothes you've packed and are comfortable for walking.

Don't leave this jewelry at home!

Another important "accessory" to wear is a medical identification bracelet or necklace, especially if you have other medical conditions in addition to your ostomy, or a continent diversion (such as an Indiana Pouch or Kock Pouch) with which other health care professionals may be unfamiliar. Remember, if you or your traveling companion is unable to converse with health care professionals, they can't tell the difference between a continent urinary diversion and an ileal conduit just by looking at it! The lack of such vital information can lead to serious medical problems.

Keep Medical Supplies with You

One thing that doesn't belong in your suit-case is your ostomy supplies—pack them separately in a carry-on bag and DON'T CHECK IT. It's highly likely that you and your luggage might not arrive at the same destination at the same time. Not having access to your ostomy supplies can cause enormous anxiety and upheaval—and can ruin your trip.

In addition to your name and address, place a card that says "Medical Supplies" on the inside of the case. This might ease passing through security checks and assist in avoiding embarrassing questions during customs inspections.

Carry a medical card with you (such as the one included with this book) or get a signed letter from your doctor on his letter-head stationery describing your medical condition and a list of all active medications and their doses (using generic names of drugs) and a list of ostomy supplies you use. If you're going out of the country, it's even more beneficial to have this letter translated into the official language of the country you're visiting. Keep the letter with you at all times.

Get a prescription for an anti-diarrhea or constipation medication should you need it away from home. Take along more than enough of any regular medications and equipment that you might need. Keep prescriptions in their original containers, and if possible, divide each medication into two watertight vials in case one is lost.

Be Prepared

With or without an ostomy, any trip—business, pleasure, or necessity—requires a little research and some extra planning. In the past, people with disabilities were seriously limited in their ability to travel far from home. Today, federal and international regulations make traveling for people with disabilities and special medical needs much simpler. Check with your insurance carrier to see if you have health coverage, especially if you are going out of the country. You may need to purchase extended coverage, or traveler's insurance.

Don't use a trip or a holiday as a time to try out new ostomy supplies. It's not wise to leave home with ostomy supplies without the confidence that they will work for you and provide a sustained and reliable wear-time.

Take a list of medical suppliers, United Ostomy Association chapters, and ET Nurses at your destination; The appendices in this book will provide you with much of the information you need. Make sure you also have the names and phone numbers of your own physicians and ET Nurses at home so you can contact them in the event of an emergency.

The Internet provides several helpful resources for people traveling with disabilities, including the names of doctors in foreign countries who speak English and have some Western medical training.

At the Airport

Airplane cabins are notoriously dry, so, the longer the flight the greater your chances of becoming dehydrated—especially if you have an ileostomy or jejunostomy. Not only can dehydration cause medical problems, but it also contributes to jet lag. Take some non-carbonated fruit juice or sports drink with you and drink some every hour or so during the flight. Plain water only doesn't replace the vital sodium and potassium you lose in your ostomy output as well as that lost in the drying atmosphere in the cabin, so you need to drink fluids other than water. Avoid alcohol as it increases dehydration.

If you suffer from motion sickness, take an over-the-counter (approved by your doctor) or prescription medication to combat it.

It's best to empty your pouch before boarding the plane. Once onboard, the cabin crews begin beverage service shortly after the "Fasten Seat Belt" sign is turned off, and the serving cart can block access to the onboard bathrooms for quite a while. Most airline terminals around the world have restrooms specifically designed for use by people with special needs. These are usually designated by the international disabled symbol and are larger than average, wheelchair accessible, and often have sinks inside the stall. However, if you need to empty your pouch during flight and the aisles are blocked, alert the cabin crew and they will make accommodations for you to get to the bathroom. Should you need a wheelchair, remember that airlines will put an onboard wheelchair on most flights upon request with a 48-hour advanced notice. You should confirm that a wheelchair will be made available to you with your carrier when you book your flight.

Traveling in a Wheelchair

For those of you in wheelchairs, a little extra planning before you leave home can make or break a business trip or vacation. You should have a maintenance check done on your equipment in advance, and take along some basic tools and extra parts just in case something breaks. Keep your ostomy supplies in your hand luggage, including extra long drainage tubing in case you have difficulty getting close enough to the toilet to empty your pouch. Also take something like a disposable wipe or towelette you can use to wash your hands after emptying. Make sure to wear clothing that's comfortable and provides easy access to your stoma—especially in tight and unfamiliar quarters.

La Dolce Vita

So, get out there. Go somewhere. Get out of Dodge! A little common sense, a sense of humor, and some preplanning are all you need to enrich the new life that ostomy surgery has given you. YES YOU CAN! In the immortal words of one of the greatest physicians for our souls, Dr. Seuss:

So. . .
Be your name Buxbaum or Bixby or Bray or
Mordecai Ali Van Allen O'Shea,
You're off to Great Places!
Today is your day!
Your mountain is waiting.
So. . . get on your way!![8]

What to include in your medical supply kit

Allow for increased usage (decreased wear time) when calculating the quantity of supplies you take.

- ✔ Scissors
- ✔ Tape
- ✔ Pouches (allow for increased usage and

[8] Dr. Seuss, *Oh, The Places You'll Go!* (New York: Random House, 1990).

decreased wear time)

✔ Solid skin barrier

✔ Skin barrier powder

✔ Skin barrier paste

✔ Adhesive remover (preferably in packets)

✔ Skin protection (preferably in packets)

✔ Deodorizer (pouch or oral tablets)

✔ Soap or skin cleanser

✔ Extra new tail closures

✔ Zip-lock bags for disposing soiled pouches

✔ Pre-moistened towels, extra tissues, disposable washcloths (in case there are none in public restrooms) NOTE: Avoid baby wipes containing oils as they will interfere with pouch adherence

✔ Air freshener or spray

✔ Ostomy appliance belts

✔ Additional special needs supplies:

✔ Powdered or liquid juices or sports drinks or other supplements

✔ Extra long drainage tubing for urostomy

✔ Leg or thigh bag or night drainage bag or bottle for urostomy

✔ Colostomy irrigation equipment and extra "security" or closed-end pouches

✔ Wheelchair accessories and extra parts

More Suggestions on What to Bring

Aliza Yaffe, RN
Preparing For the Trip

To fully enjoy your trip, I recommend a few preparations.

It is a good idea to carry a short medical report on the type of surgery you had and any additional treatments and a list of medications that you are currently taking. If you have any other medical condition it should be mentioned in the report. It is important that the report be in English, even when traveling from or to a non-English speaking country.

Your ET nurse may supply you with a travel card, if not, one is included in this book. A travel card may be valuable in avoiding embarrassing situations in airports and customs. Travel cards typically include the following information:

- ✔ A summary of your medical report
- ✔ The specific type of stoma you have
- ✔ Allergies
- ✔ Special diet requirements
- ✔ A statement mentioning that you have a medical condition that requires you to carry appliances and supplies
- ✔ A statement indicating that if a body search is required, it should be carried out by a health professional

Your ET nurse will also provide you with the addresses of ostomy organizations in the places you plan to visit. It is possible to get an up-to-date list in the International Ostomy Organization web site at www.ostomyinterna-tional.org. Having this information will give you an additional sense of security knowing that help is available to you if you need it.

First Aid Kit

Your first aid kit should have:

- ✔ Simple pain medication that you are comfortable taking for headache, pain or fever
- ✔ Anti-diarrhea medication such as Imodium
- ✔ Water purifying pills or liquid when traveling to places where the water supply safety is questionable
- ✔ Bandages, creams, ointments
- ✔ Extra ostomy supplies

CHAPTER FIVE

You Won't Unravel When You Travel

TIPS FOR TRIPS

By Micki Gelman

So you're an ostomate. And you want to travel but you're scared shitless. You think your pouch will leak or your flange will fall off or you won't find a bathroom or you'll smell or the airlines will lose your ostomy supplies. If want to hear that none of the above will happen, this would be a fairy tale. When you're an ostomate, anything can happen at the worst time. Whoever heard of a terrific time for your pouch to pop off? For your flange to flood over? Not to worry. You can overcome everything that happens and clean anything that falls out or falls off. And there's more good news because I've never heard of anyone who went to ostomy heaven because their pouch leaked. Nor has any ostomate that I know been thrown out of a county or country due to smelling or expelling gas.

As a columnist for the *OSTOMY QUARTERLY*, my brain is bursting with travel information. When you read the Tips for Trips later in this chapter, most are from ostomates who read the column. From all the letters I've received, no one ever wrote about running out of equipment en route to anywhere nor has anyone reported that their trip was terrible.

No sir, folks. Ostomates travel. They go on cruises, they hike, camp, go river rafting, fly to jungles, go fishing, mountain climbing, scuba diving, visit foreign countries, and some are brave enough for bungee jumping. However, they plan carefully before taking the burro trip from the rim of the Grand Canyon to the bottom. They find out how long a hot air balloon will be flying before they book a ride. Not all would opt to climb that spiral staircase in the Statue of Liberty. Some ostomates won't budge without an accessible bathroom; others opt to go anywhere.

The bottom line on travel is that when you plan well, you will survive mishaps and still have a wonderful time. How do I know? Why am I so sure? Because I've been on trips where nothing happened and on trips where everything happened. I've lived through leaks, suffered with swollen stomas, pouches

popping off, suspicious airport security ques-
tioning the bulge in my slacks, and countless
inconveniences.

Yet, I still travel. Why? Because I feel that
no adversity should halt adventure. When I
became a colostomate, I was determined to
have a normal life. Therefore, when travel
brochures to cruise the West Indies crept into
my mailbox, the trip took over my brain. The
pictures were colorful and exciting and allur-
ing, and I had never cruised. This type of trip
seemed ideal. There would be a bathroom in
my cabin and more bathrooms on every deck.
So my partner and I plunked down our
money and booked a cabin for a cruise to the
Caribbean. And the West Indies was wonderful until we were strolling down the street on
a sunny day in Martinique. Suddenly, my
pouch started filling so I started asking about
bathrooms in every store. I found none. My
pouch didn't know that and as it got fuller, I
began to panic. With no bathroom plumbing
in sight I realized that this idyllic island had
become an ostomate's nightmare. As I walked
with my hand beneath my pouch to give it
support from the weight of loose feces, I wondered: would it or wouldn't it fall off when it
was so full? My partner quietly suggested we
return to our ship. Although the dock was
blocks away, there was no alternative. Nor was
I hopeful because the weight of the pouch
told me it would overflow before I got to the
ship. I was ecstatic when I spotted a store-

front with a small sign "American Embassy" over the door. Without hesitation, we went inside where a uniformed man with a French accent greeted us graciously in broken English. After I told him what I wanted, he frowned and said, "No. Not poh-see-blez." "Emergency!" I sputtered. Towering over me, he shook his head, "No pub-leek." The full pouch was pushing its luck, making me crazy. Wasn't I an American citizen in an American embassy? Wasn't I asking to use an American toilet? Wasn't that American toilet bought with my American tax money?

What gave this French-speaking West Indian officer authority to forbid me to use an American toilet? While I doubted that he knew an ostomy from an oyster, I nevertheless brazenly unzipped my slacks as I muttered about writing my congressman. Showing him my pouch, he stared, blinked, nodded, and pointed to the direction of the bathroom.

That's the incident that taught me never to leave home without locating a lavatory. That means anywhere. Not only the Caribbean, but wherever you travel whether it's two miles or two thousand. Know where toilets are in Tanganyika, or Tokyo, or the tennis courts where you play; the supermarket you frequent or any museum you meander in; your high school stadium or Yankee Stadium.

That's worth repeating. If you need a bathroom to prevent pouch explosion, don't leave home until you know the accessibility of a bathroom, no matter where you're headed. And any ostomate who settles for one of those metal portable potties, pray it has water. Why bring your buns to a small cell that's usually smelly, dirty and dark? You need to see what you're doing.

Another step to becoming a happy traveler is to pack sufficient supplies. That means taking double the amount you normally use. When you fly, never check equipment with your luggage. When you drive, never put pouches or flanges or any equipment in your trunk. Staying with you, supplies will never be lost, overheated, frozen or stolen. This rule applies to any means of transportation like a train, bus, burro, hot air balloon, camel caravan, kayak—you get the idea. Can you really go anywhere? Sure, if you have the money, any trip is possible. However, plan ahead. Mountain climbing is okay only if you can change your pouch dangling from a rope. Are you a camper? The facilities are rustic so go where there are plenty of big bushes. Now let's get back to supplies. Anyone going to a location where you can't get equipment should forget about taking a duplicate amount—in that situation you need supplies in triplicate. Always carry toilet paper and baby wipes whether you go to Montana or Morocco or Mexico. One reason is that when you're absorbed with sightseeing, you'll be concerned about snapping shots of scenery. Want to bet you'll forget to check the toilet paper supply before you go into that stall with stingy space? It's no fun fumbling without water to clean the tail of that pouch after it's empty.

Another reason is the unpredictability of what can happen when you use a toilet away from home. For instance, during a trip to Mexico after walking blocks, I finally found public toilets that were nothing but narrow wooden stalls. Instead of a door for each stall, privacy was provided by a gauze curtain held in place by a flimsy string. Inside the stall, I discovered there was not a shred of toilet paper. As a new ostomate, I wasn't wise about toting a ton of tissues so I was stuck without cleanup material. To get toilet tissue, I had to ask for it from the toilet paper lady who was a middle aged Spanish senora with a somber look on her face. She sat in front of the string of toilets, holding a piece of frayed cardboard with 25 cents printed unevenly in red crayon. Beside her on the ground were three rolls of coarse toilet paper. After I walked over to her and said. "I want toilet paper," she pointed to her sign. When I gave her a quarter, she tore off one square. "I want more," I said. The toilet paper lady held out her hand. I gave her another 25 cents. I got one more square. This was unbelievable! Each time I put a quarter in her hand, she handed me one square. That bathroom break cost me over five dollars.

No one can predict what will happen, we can only try to foresee what might happen and prevent problems. For example, when traveling by plane, get help putting your suitcase in the overhead luggage space. Sure, I know you think you're strong enough to lift a hundred horses, but you're an ostomate now. Therefore, remind yourself that you're not just lifting a suitcase. Sometimes you have to shove another suitcase to the side to make room for your own. Lifting and stretching to deal with luggage in the overhead could loosen your flange.

Standard practice before you get on a train, plane, bus, boat, canoe, or kayak is to empty your pouch and check and your equipment. Make sure your flange is adhering and your pouch is solidly attached to the flange. If I sound picky and finicky, blame it on the bathroom battle I had returning from a conference in Las Vegas. When the sign flashed that we could move around the cabin, as I stood up to go to the bathroom, I found myself in misery and muck as my pouch popped loose from the flange. And since my colostomy thinks it's an ileostomy, watery feces immediately started trickling down my leg.

With only three rows separating me from the bathroom, all I could think was to get there fast. Once inside that miniscule stall, I realized I could do nothing without my supplies sitting under the seat in front of where I sat. Sticking my head out the bathroom door, I signaled to a flight attendant, explained what had happened and asked her to bring my supplies.

Clutching the carry-on, I locked the door, gritted my teeth and pinched myself to see if this was for real. When I didn't wake up in my warm dry bed in New Mexico, I knew I had big trouble. Did you every try to move around in one of those mini bathrooms?

First, I took the flange and pouch out of my slacks and put them on the sink. I'd wrap them for disposal later. Next, I had to remove my slacks, which were filled with feces. But I had a problem because I only had one free hand. The other one was still clutching the carry-on filled with supplies. Where could I put it? I looked around for a flat surface. The toilet was of no use so I put the lid down and used that. Due to the cramped space, even though I'm slender, there was zero room for maneuvering. As I stripped off slacks, more feces spread on both of my legs, on the straps of my sandals, between my toes, and onto the floor. I was filthier than when I started. There were also feces on the wall behind me, in front of me, and on the door. Shaking my head in disbelief, I blinked back tears telling myself there was no time to cry and no room for tears in that tiny space. Then I turned on the faucet in the mini sink and cursed worse than a seasick sailor as a trickle of cold water dripped out. Slowly, I cleaned my slacks in sections as well as I could. I held my nylon underwear under the wisps of water and tossed my hose in the paper towel disposal. Finally, I ran my sandals under the stream of water, grabbed paper towels to blot them dry and propped them up on end on the sink. Standing barefoot and half naked, I had to make a decision. The slacks, which were new and cost over $40 were a mess. How would I get them home? Searching though the carry—on, there were no extra plastic bags. But my clean clothes were in a waterproof bag so I took them out and stuffed in the soiled slacks and underwear. Then I realized I had to clean the bathroom before I got dressed or I'd get feces all over myself as I moved around in the cramped space. I blessed the plentiful supply of paper towels because there were feces to clean from the sink, the floor and door, walls and mirror. The process was slow with the tiny trickle of cold water. Without room to maneuver, I had to be careful. If I cleaned one wall and bumped into the opposite one, I'd have more feces on me. Finally, it was done.

As I looked at the fresh slacks and under-wear, I was grateful to whoever warned me to take extra clothes in the event of an accident. Despite the difficulty of moving my long legs in that cramped space, I managed to get into the clean underwear, slacks, and sandals. I stuffed he plastic bag of soiled clothes in the carry—on, zipped it tightly, and rechecked the cubbyhole bathroom for feces I might have missed. With the dim lighting, it was hard to see so I wiped off the rim of the sink and gave the floor an extra swipe. Finally finished, I turned on the faucet with the trickle of water, splashed my sweaty face, reapplied make up, combed my hair, and looked at my watch. I saw dried feces. After cleaning the dial, I realized I'd been in the bathroom over thirty minutes. Embarrassment overcame me as I wondered what the other passengers would think when I finally emerged from the bathroom and returned to my seat. What had they done with their bulging bladders all that time?

I hesitated about opening the door. During all that time no one had knocked on the door to use the bathroom. I didn't know whether the flight attendant understood what an ostomy is, but I realized passengers must have been directed to another bathroom. Since I had to return to my seat, I unlocked the door, turned the knob, stepped into the aisle, and looked at the people on the plane. I was stunned at what I saw. They were the same as they were when I went into the bathroom. Some were reading, some sleeping—no one was looking at the bathroom waiting for me to emerge. They seemingly couldn't care less. As I fell into my seat, my partner raised his eyebrows. All I said was "Don't ask," and he didn't.

Do I still fly? You bet, but I check my flange frequently (at least five times) before boarding. I also use a new product in my pouch that thickens loose stools. My emergency supplies still include a change of clothing plus a washcloth, soap, and paper towels. I also found that problems might occur no matter what you choose as a mode of transportation, including the family car.

To attend a family wedding only 450 miles away in Denver, my partner and I decided to drive there from New Mexico. A day before we were scheduled to leave, late in the afternoon, the weather report announced a storm for the Rocky Mountain area. That meant the highway patrol could close icy roads over the mountain passes. If that happened we'd be stuck on the wrong side of the mountain and miss the wedding. Without delay, we packed the car and departed for Denver to get there before the storm. As we approached northern New Mexico, we ran into light snow, and by midnight when we were on Raton Pass, we found ourselves in a raging snowstorm with no visibility. Did you guess that's when my colostomy bag got full? Although I was prepared to empty en route, to do so, we had to stop the car. While some colostomates can change pouches in a moving car, I cannot. For me, changing a pouch requires two feet on terra firma. That terra firma can be in a bathroom, a desert or rooftop. Cars moving through a snowstorm with their wheels on solid ground don't count. Have you ever tried to stop your car in a snowstorm when you can't see the road or the median or the shoulder? As long as we followed the taillights of the truck ahead we felt safe. Unfortunately, colostomies don't know about snowstorms and zero visibility and, therefore, make monstrous demands. Realizing we had no options, we waited until we saw a road sign on the right, then veered off the road knowing we'd be off the highway when we were on the other side of the sign.

Slick roads ruined our plans. We hit the sign that dented the door and sideswiped the car as the wheels slid on ice before we could stop. Opening the car door, I got out, and at 2:30 a.m., in the dark, in freezing temperatures and blowing snow, I unzipped my parka and shoved down my slacks. With frozen fingers, I removed the overflowing pouch, plunked it in a plastic bag, cleaned around the stoma with a moist tissue, put on a fresh pouch, swept snow off my middle, and pulled up my pants. Do I still travel by car? You bet I do. I refuse to let my stoma stagnate my life. Although I learned a lot, as savvy as I had become, a new kind of problem kept cropping up. When I was in an out-of-town mall, bathroom facilities were often far from where I was shopping, and most shops had no public restroom. The polite question, "May I use your bathroom?" got me the polite answer, "We don't have a public bathroom."

In my family, my father and several relatives owned stores. Having grown up in a store, I knew every establishment had a bathroom. So I considered what would convince me to allow a stranger into this sacred space off limits. When I had the answer, I tested it in a fancy Phoenix boutique and a San Francisco shoe salon. Being a generous person, I'll share the solution.

When you must absolutely empty your pouch, ask for the store manager. When that prestigious person arrives, you adopt a confidential manner and say: "I have a medical emergency and must use your bathroom." Trust me. Would I lie to you? I've never been refused. How do you get your ostomy through security in foreign airports? This one's not easy, and I found the answer from a female ileostomate we'll call Helen who related a harrowing experience. There she was in Asia when a buzzer went off during a security check. When Helen was ordered to remove her appliance, she tried to explain she couldn't do that. She grew frantic as inspectors, who couldn't understand her problem, insisted on seeing what was under the appliance. Fortunately, a doctor who knew the language heard the ruckus and knowing what was happening, he intervened and wrote "medical prosthesis" in the language of the country Helen was visiting. All of that tells you that before leaving this country, get the translation of "medical prosthesis" in the language of each country you'll be passing through. Keep those wonderful words with your passport. Memorizing them might also help.

Going through customs inspection, it helps to have a letter from your doctor listing all the medicine you carry. You're allowed anything prescribed for personal use. The letter should halt hassles from officials who are concerned about drug traffic. If you're getting the idea that traveling as an ostomate takes courage, you're right. When you're starting out, it's scary. You need all the help and hints you can get.

TIPS FOR TRIPS

- ✔ Be prepared for emergencies. Remember Murphy's Law: Anything that can go wrong will go wrong.
- ✔ Do you remember reading several pages back to take two to three times as many supplies as you'll need? I'm repeating it because it's that important.
- ✔ When you pack your supplies, put everything out that you use. Mentally, go through the procedure of changing your equipment to make sure you have it all.
- ✔ It won't hurt a thing to put a few small strong rubber bands in your wallet. Those are your lifesavers in case the tail clip on your flange collapses.
- ✔ As you pack, separate liquids from tape, pouches and flanges. Leak is a four-letter dirty word in the ostomy world. The

last thing you want is wet film for your camera.

✔ When packing your supplies, don't just grab a box of pouches and a fistful of flanges. Supplies should come from several boxes. Do you need five flanges? Take them from three different boxes. Ditto for pouches—if you need 10 pouches, take them from three boxes. This will protect you from a predicament of sailing through the South Seas and finding you're stuck with a full box of flanges that lost their stick 'um.

✔ The day before starting your trip, change your equipment to make sure nothing leaks. Usually, a defect becomes apparent within 24 hours.

✔ Carry all your standard equipment in one case plus emergency supplies for an unexpected change in a fanny bag, camera case or pocketbook. Emergency supplies should include zip-top baggies for disposal of equipment, baby wipes or a few paper towels to wet before you go into a public cubbyhole toilet so you'll have something resembling water to help you clean up.

✔ Emergency equipment is a personal matter. Whatever becomes necessary should be included. On extended trips when you can't carry all your supplies, check with your ostomy distributor or write the chapter in the area where you'll be for places to buy your supplies.

✔ Never entrust your supplies to anyone. Don't check them when you're going by train, plane, boat or bus. Sure, I said this one before, but it's important enough to repeat. Supplies buried in the belly of a cargo compartment can't help you.

✔ Ostomates taking a trip by car should have their supplies inside the car. Another repetition? Right, because it's another *must*. That trunk could get too hot in summer—which can damage appliances, dry out cement, melt or cause tubes to expand or explode. The trunk can also get too cold in the winter, and you'll freak out with frozen flanges.

✔ Some ostomates buy special cases for their supplies, making sure the dimensions fit airline specifications as a carry-on. Whatever you use to carry supplies should be waterproof and large enough to accommodate all your supplies.

✔ Travelers also say it's a good idea to get ready for your next trip as soon as you get home. Unpack your special ostomy case or carry-on. Check your supplies, replenish whatever you need, add items you forgot to take, include new items you decided to take, and put a note in your case with the date you repacked. That date will clue you to take new medications or supplies that you started using recently.

✔ Worried about leaking in that strange bed? Visit your favorite discount or department store and buy a waterproof mattress pad. If a regular size waterproof pad is too bulky to pack, ask for a crib size that you can put on top of the sheet. A flannel back tablecloth can be used to protect a mattress from leaks, but it's harder to keep straight when you change positions during the night.

✔ No room for a pad? Large plastic bags will protect a mattress and fit easily in a small case. The disadvantage is that they're uncomfortable to sleep on. Placed on top of a sheet, plastic slides around on the bed, and you'll finally force yourself to get up in the middle of the night to put the plastic bag under the sheet. Remember, if you're going to a warm climate, plastic will make you even hotter when sleeping in summer.

✔ For visiting in the home of someone you know really well, like your son or daughter or mom or favorite aunt, just tell them you might leak and ask them to do whatever they feel necessary to protect the mattress.

✔ Include a copy of the United Ostomy Association chapter directory in case you need assistance getting emergency supplies.

✔ Since medical information could be essential in an emergency, carry identification specifying your type of ostomy and the equipment you use: the name and phone number of the manufacturer, the style and size numbers. If necessary, the manufacturer could mail supplies to you. If none of the above works and you need supplies, look in the yellow pages of the phone book under Surgical Supplies.

✔ If you don't wear a medical ID such as a bracelet or necklace, what are you waiting for? Run to your nearest drug store and order one. A medical card such as the one included in this book would also be helpful, should you have an emergency.

✔ If you can't sleep with a light on (to check your ostomy in the wee hours), take a night light to use in your hotel (or motel or mother-in-law's). Put a note in your suitcase so you won't leave it behind.

✔ No night light? Take a small flashlight. Is there one on your key ring? Use that.

✔ Ileostomates and colostomates generally change their pouches everyday when traveling. Before the trip, they accumulate recycled pouches so they don't have to be concerned about cleaning them.

✔ Save your plastic grocery bags and take enough so you can dispose of your used pouches in a plastic sack and tie the top to conceal odors. These can be put in any wastebasket. You can also use aluminum foil for disposal of used equipment. A sheet 10 inches long wrapped around used equipment can be folded flat to a four-inch square and discarded in any receptacle.

✔ If you like to use foil, you'll love it more when you buy foil sheets, which snap out one at a time. A box of 500 costs about $10 which figures to two cents each and should last a long time.

✔ While sightseeing each day, take an extra flange and pouch with you. Knowing you can replace this equipment on the spot gives you the freedom and confidence to schedule an all-day tour.

✔ In hot weather, put protection between your pouch and skin to prevent a skin rash.

✔ Did you forget to pack pouch covers for the above? Then take yourself to a store where you can buy baby bibs—drug stores, discount stores, and supermarkets carry inexpensive baby items. Pick out some bibs with lining under the plastic. Put the bib between your pouch and skin, loop the ties around the top of your pouch and tie them together.

✔ During your trip, on those quickie bathroom breaks, keep track of your pouch clip by tucking it in your watchband or the top of your sock or shoe. If you don't wear a watch and are barefoot, females can put the pouch clip in their bras; for men, that clip could go in a shirt pocket.

✔ Urostomates on long car trips can hook their bag to the drainage container. For safety, you can put the drainage container in a wastebasket.

✔ Urostomates need large plastic bags that zip closed for bedside overnight drainage. Use a clothespin to attach the bag to a wastebasket, then zip closed to the drain tube.

✔ Lots of ostomates find it convenient to wear shirts and pants that open in the front when emptying.

✔ Men can use suspenders to hold up drainage containers. Most urostomates put their drainage containers in some type of basin to prevent overflow on carpets wherever they're staying.

✔ Car travelers: whenever you stop to empty your pouch, take toilet paper and moist wipes with you. Many roadside facilities offer a toilet that flushes and nothing more.

✔ Wherever you are in this world, when you see a bathroom, use it to empty your pouch. Forget about being in a hurry. Slow down, and don't press your luck in strange places. That next bathroom could be a half-day or 300 miles away.

✔ For extra safety, you can picture-frame your appliance. This means you get waterproof tape about one inch wide. Cut four strips of tape the length of your flange; paste one strip of tape around each side of your flange, framing it like a picture.

✔ Yes, you can swim with your appliance on. Put your equipment on at least 24 hours before you go in the water. Then plunk yourself in a bathtub with your appliance submerged in the water for about 15 minutes to make sure it's sticking. Don't just sit in the tub watching to see if the flange falls off. Wiggling around and stretching in the water helps simulate actual swimming.

✔ If you spring a leak when it's impossible to change equipment, a Band Aid or piece of medical tape can temporarily stop the leak.

✔ Irrigate with drinking water only. Whenever you hesitate to put the water in your mouth, it shouldn't go in your stoma. No exceptions!

✔ To hang your bag while irrigating away from home, take shower hooks that snap together like safety pins, make a chain the length you need and loop it over the shower rod.

✔ While camping out or hiking or flying or sightseeing, you can carry an extra flange and pouch in a fanny pouch.

✔ Those who wear two-piece equipment should try one-piece equipment for travel. Many ostomates find it more convenient and like the idea of not worrying about the pouch separating from the flange.

✔ Ileostomates can carry a small plastic bottle and fill it with water before going into the bathroom cubicle. Those few ounces of water should be enough to clean up a messy tail. Wet wipes will also work.

✔ Keep your body from dehydrating by drinking enough water. Is food a problem? Wherever you are, find a grocery store, buy what you need and pack a lunch.

Experiment at home with whatever you think will work. Never mind that no other ostomate you know does what you're doing. If it works, use it. Be open for new experiences. To illustrate, I'll relate what happened to a new ileostomate, a 38-year-old engineer, who went to Jamaica with his four friends and their wives. Every day the group would swim, then sit in a hot tub. Although "Justin" swam and sunbathed with the group, he refused to soak in the hot tub because he'd been told his equipment would come off. On the last afternoon as Justin was reading in the sun, one of his friends asked, "Do you take a hot shower in that stuff you have to wear?" As Justin nodded yes, his friends lifted him in his patio chair, trotted to the hot tub, and yelled, "And a-one, and a-two, and a-three, and into the sea!" and tossed him in.

What did he do? "I stayed in," Justin said, "and my flange stayed on. Don't believe anyone who tells you hot tubs are off limits." I can't think of anything off limits. Don't shake your head thinking that's impossible until you read about a hiker who was wheeled into surgery with a tag on his toe—it was a note to the scrub nurse so she wouldn't wash off the circle where he wanted his stoma. It was an important note because the hiker wore hip belts.

If you think those hip belts are only for hiking equipment, you're wrong. And if you think this hiker meandered up the mountains only in warm weather, you're about to discover what real colostomates really do. During the winter, he packs extra supplies in one hip belt. At night, he puts them in his sleeping bag and explains, "It's not good to let the wafers freeze so I stick them in my coat pocket in zero-degree weather." How does this hiker clean his pouch in freezing weather? Does he search the mountain to find a cabin with a bathroom and warm water? Not our hero. He says, "At 20 degrees above zero, evacuation of the pouch is difficult because the waste is 'stiff.' I found it's worth waiting until midday and in the sunlight to clean the pouch. If duty calls in the evening, evacuating in front of a campfire into a plastic bag that snaps closed is best. Burn the toilet paper and the waste, too, if you're among friends.

"Never, never, never try to bury used supplies. Burn them completely in a good fire or haul them home in a plastic bag. Since I'm not a pouch washer, I clean out the end of the pouch with toilet paper. In cold weather that can be pesky because the wind or temperature causes the waste to dry before you can clean up. That's when a dab of water or snow can complete the job."

With water supplies and temperatures uncertain, this experienced hiker doesn't recommend irrigation. He suggests taking extra supplies. For clothing, he advises hikers to cut the pockets out of hiking shorts and nylon wind pants so your hip belt can be "threaded" through the openings and fastened under the pouch. Take care so it doesn't rub the wafer loose.

He warns against keeping supplies in the sun in the summer, spring, and fall. That sounds like something you've heard before in this chapter. Does that convince you to follow directions?

As for niceties, they still apply even in the wilds of winter. He says, "I usually hike at the back of a group so I can release gas from the pouch without fuss or comment. My tent has no floor, just a fancy tarp so ventilation is not a problem." For indoor people, that means passing gas won't leave an odor because the airflow is continuous in a tent with no floor.

Our hero, the hiker, also says, "If I were

in a tent with a floor, out of respect for my tent mate, I'd get up and go outside to vent the pouch if necessary." That could be at 9 p.m. or 3:45 a.m. in temperatures above or below zero. If you're getting a mental picture of a 30-something jock, you're wrong. He's 57.

There seems to be nothing to stop an ostomate with plans to travel. One colostomate, with no time to get to a bathroom to let gas out of his ballooning pouch, stuck a pin through his trousers and into the top of his pouch as he boarded the plane. It worked. Another elderly gentleman with poor eyesight who liked to attend golf tournaments was upset because he felt he couldn't attend a golf tournament without his wife. She always helped him position his equipment but couldn't travel with him. Wanting to go to an invitational tournament, he was depressed and thought hard about how he could see his equipment and be independent. Finally, he propped a mirror so he could see his flange and made ink marks on his abdomen where his flange should go. Then he marched to the local tattoo parlor and had those marks put permanently on his tummy.

When it comes to traveling:

✔ I don't know any place an ostomate can't go.

✔ I don't know any challenge an ostomate can't overcome.

✔ There are guidelines galore about how to travel. But there's nothing about travel limits.

✔ Why? There aren't any so make your plans and pack your clothes because you won't unravel when you travel!

Bon voyage!

And More Tips...
Candida Carvalheira, President
Sociedade Brasileira dos Ostomiizados's

International Trips:
✔ Request that passport should identify an ostomate to help police when they search personal belongings.

✔ Due to ignorance, Customs officials might take an ostomate for a drug addict or middleman (drug mule).

✔ Reserve seats near restrooms just in case of emergencies and we need to change pouches.

✔ When on long trips by bus, advise driver that there is an ostomate on board. We need to use the restroom on the way.

✔ Verify that you have packed your pouches in your personal hand luggage.

"Duplicate Your Prescriptions"
Larry Trapp
United States

I always take my ostomy appliances with me on the plane. That way, I know they won't get lost in transit. I have traveled so much, and I have never had any problems. I take along an ample supply of appliances because I would rather have too many than not enough. I have had tetanus and Small Pox vaccines as a precaution. I take several medications, so I had a duplicate copy of all my prescriptions signed by both of my doctors for the purpose of safely getting through customs. I even bring an extra prescription for my glasses!

"Practical Advice"
Linda and Ken Aukett
Ileostomy, United States

✔ Remember that everyone smells and makes noise in the bathroom so don't worry unduly about that. Above all, keep doing what you love rather than letting the ostomy keep you home!

✔ You might want to carry one or two of the seat covers that are sometimes provided in "better" toilets (at least in ladies' rooms).

✔ Have a hanky or something handy that can be folded up to wedge the door closed since sometimes doors won't stay closed by themselves.

✔ If you're using drainable pouches, all you need to do is sit and open the drain end (and find a safe spot for the clip). Put a few sheets of toilet paper on the surface of the water to cut splashing and noise. A few sheets of toilet paper on the front inner surface of airplane toilets will help when it is time to flush.

✔ If you don't have a drainable pouch, you can get collapsible cups that can be unfolded, filled with water and used to wash out a closed pouch. Another option is a squeeze bottle.

✔ One-piece pouches can be removed and put into opaque bags (available from ostomy supply houses—or recycle a bread wrapper or store bag).

Odor control can be easy—your supplier probably has small aerosol containers of odor-neutralizing products. Anywhere except an airplane, you can light a couple of matches or a candle to conceal the smell.

Medical Identification Jewelry
Bobb L. Courtman

People have always worn special identification that openly linked them to their social, spiritual or political status. This custom started thousands of years ago. Perhaps it began with the shape of a wooden totem or the color of a tattoo. No one knows. We do know that the tradition still exists. Take a look at religious groups, street gangs, the military and fraternal societies.

The widespread use of special medical identification originated with the Army's dog tags in WWII. These tags were made of stainless steel. The wearer's blood type and a religious preference (for burial reasons) were reverse-embossed onto the tag, which made the information permanent.

Today, personalized medical identification is no longer limited to the military. It has become an extremely important emergency-alert device used by thousands of people around the world. Rather than indicating your social or political status, medical identification tells others of your medical status.

For many people, wearing emergency medical ID is not an option. Those of us that have had surgical procedures or implants such as an ostomy or pacemaker have to wear it. If you have a chronic illness like diabetes, or life-threatening allergies such as an allergy to penicillin or latex, emergency medical identification could save your life.

EMS and EMT personnel are trained to look for medical emergency identification on all four limbs and the neck. If you cannot speak for yourself, your medical ID can tell emergency medical personnel what to treat first. Precious time can be saved and unnecessary treatment avoided.

All medical identification jewelry or cards should contain a clear image of the caduceus,

162

162 YES WE CAN!YES WE CAN!

which is the universal symbol for medicine. The caduceus is the familiar staff with two intertwined snakes and wings at the top. Originally, it was an emblem of the Greco-Roman god of medicine (or healing) named Aesculapius. The US Army made it their official insignia for members of the medical corps 50 years ago. Now, it is the most recognized medical symbol in the world.

No one wants to wear emergency medical jewelry. We would all be much happier if we didn't have any illness at all. No one wears medical jewelry if they are in "good health." So, to take some of the unpleasantness out of wearing the boring medical jewelry you find at the drug store, there are several companies recommended in Appendix VI that offer a broad selection of medical-ID jewelry in 14k gold and sterling silver. If you have to wear it, do it with style. Don't settle for a piece of jewelry that makes you feel like a tagged animal.

CHAPTER SIX

Nutrition

Aliza Yaffe, RN

In the days of the Bible, people traveled in the quest of food, as did Jacob's sons when they traveled to Egypt. The modern traveler does not direct himself to a far away place because of hunger; he does so in search of pleasure, adventure or business.

In food we search for more than just answering to the essential need of supplying our bodies with the necessary energy it needs. We eat to answer to social, emotional and cultural needs. We enjoy eating in the company of other people and many of our social activities include meals at home or away. We spend a significant amount of our time buying, preparing and consuming food.

Who wants to travel to a far away place and not be able to taste the different flavors it offers? Part of any vacation is adventuring

with different food. That is true for everybody, including people with ostomies.

This chapter will deal with some facts on
the influence of different food items on the
functioning of the stoma and some tips and
advice will be provided in order to help make
vacationing a positive experience.

Facts on Nutrition

Remember that eating is one of life's greatest pleasures. We select our foods according
to our environment, culture, beliefs and current health condition. Our family history, the
seasons of the year, the media, health professionals, friends and other factors influence
the variety, quality and quantity of food we
eat. A balanced diet enables you to stay
healthy and feel your best. It can also help to
reduce the risks of chronic diseases, such as
heart disease or to help control others such
as diabetes. Food provides the body with
energy and mineral elements, vitamins,
amino acids, fatty acids and fiber that are
needed for proper daily function. The need
for food varies with age and level of activity.
Younger people usually need to eat more
because they tend to be more active than the
elderly. Individuals wishing to reduce their
weight need to eat less and be more active
(easier said than done!). Healthful diets contain the amounts of essential nutrients and

calories needed to prevent nutritional deficiencies and excesses.

Basic Food Categories
* Fluids (water)
* Proteins (meat, fish, dairy products, soy)
* Fats
* Fruits and vegetables
* Grains
* Carbohydrates (sugar)
* Vitamins and minerals
* Electrolytes (potassium, sodium, chloride, bicarbonate and others)

Daily servings of each group provide our bodies with the nutrients needed to function properly. Each person needs an adjusted amount of calories based on age, health status and activity. For example, a normal adult would need at least 1200 calories a day to maintain weight and a reasonable level of energy. It is very important to eat a variety of foods based on the different food categories. It is recommended to eat more grains, fruits and vegetables and less meat, fats and sweets (carbohydrates).

Fiber (roughage) is very important and is found in fruits and vegetables (especially the skins), and in full grain products such as rice, wheat and cereals. Your digestive enzymes do not affect fiber and it has very few calories. The main purpose of fiber in the diet is to aid in the transportation of stool along the intestinal tract. The amount of fiber influences stool consistency and elimination patterns. Fiber must be chewed thoroughly and should be consumed with plenty of fluids. You will need to experiment to reach your optimal amount of fiber; individuals with ostomies are no exception. Too little fiber in the diet may cause constipation, while too much may cause loose stool and gas.

Is there an Ileostomy or Colostomy diet?

An individual who has an ostomy may need to adapt his or her diet depending on the type of ostomy and its management. As a rule, there is no need for an "ostomy diet." The key is to KNOW YOUR BODY. Keep a diary for a few weeks in which you note what you eat and if it had any adverse influence on your bowel activity. After a while you will be able to easily identify which foods do not agree with you.

Some rules
- ✔ Add new foods gradually, one at a time, in order to recognize which ones do not suit you.
- ✔ Do not skip meals.
- ✔ Eat at regular intervals; some individuals find it better to eat small meals at fre-

quent intervals.
- ✔ Some persons find that drinking carbonated beverages and using straws may give them more gas.
- ✔ Drink plenty of fluids.
- ✔ Chew food completely.

Air Travel and Your Diet

Eat a light, low-fat meal prior to traveling. Some people experience more gas during air travel so be prepared with extra pouches, wet tissues, a plastic bag for disposal of used pouches and a change of underwear. If you have a left colostomy, use pouches with a filter. It is a good idea to change the whole appliance, flange and bag just before traveling; this will result in more confidence.

During the flight drink plenty of water but try to avoid alcohol. Eat lightly. Take at least one week's supply of your appliances in your hand luggage as sometimes suitcases end up in the most exotic places possible, without their legal owners.

Odor and Gas

Certain foods may increase odor and gas—remember this is an individual problem and one not everybody experiences. If a certain food has caused you a problem, maybe you should try it again—perhaps in a different combination it will suit you. The most common gas producing foods are: asparagus, broccoli, Brussels sprouts, cabbage, cauliflower, beans, nuts, onions, eggs, garlic, corn, mushrooms, peas, spinach and fish. Parsley, yogurt and buttermilk are natural deodorants and are available around the world.

Diarrhea

Diarrhea can spoil a vacation whether you have a stoma or not. It has been named Montezuma's Revenge (Mexico), Aztec Two Step (South America), Turkey Trots (Turkey), Hong Kong Dog (Hong Kong), and Delhi Belly (India) and has many other local names.

Diarrhea is usually a bacterial infection contracted by travelers that wonder why the local people do not also become ill. The most common source of infection is contaminated water or food. Drinking only bottled or boiled water can prevent this trouble. Do not use ice cubes in your drinks. Use only bottled/boiled water for brushing your teeth and irrigating your stoma. Safe fruits are those with thick peels or rinds, like oranges and bananas. Vegetables should be thoroughly cooked. This precaution is not universal and should be taken only in areas where the quality of water is not safe for drinking or where fields are irrigated with contaminated water.

The current situation of a specific country is available from the United States Center for Disease Control or at its website: www.cdc.gov/travel/index/htm.

Even when individuals take all the necessary measures, sometimes they may become a bit careless and contract diarrhea. First of all, do not panic! With proper treatment you will soon be able to return to your travel plan. Treatment for diarrhea should include drinking plenty of fluids (to prevent dehydration) and taking an anti-diarrheal medication. If the diarrhea persists, contact a doctor, preferably recommended by the local Ostomy Association or your hotel. Remember that if you had too many anti-diarrheal tablets you may have at least one day without bowel movements. Do not become anxious, as this is normal.

What do I do if I become constipated?

Constipation means insufficient, irregular evacuation of the bowels. It is a common complaint of travelers whether they have a stoma or not. It is caused by insufficient fluid intake and slow adaptation to the difference in humidity and temperature. Drinking plenty of fluids will help to prevent or alleviate constipation. Should constipation persist and you have a urostomy or colostomy, you may take a small dose of a mild stool softener, preferably recommended by your doctor. If vomiting or nausea accompanies the constipation, consult a doctor. If you have an ileostomy and your appliance remains empty, you must consult a doctor.

Special Considerations According to the Type of Stoma

Ileostomy

Fluid and electrolyte balances are important to a person with an ileostomy. Fluids are lost in the stool when the amount exceeds 750 cc per day and the consistency of the stool is watery and not like a soft paste. Moderately salted food will usually compensate for the loss of electrolytes. Dehydration may occur if the stool becomes watery and if fluids are lost by other routes such as sweating and breathing. Fluid replacement is the rule—via water, salty drinks (soups), or electrolyte replacement drinks (sport drinks). The only way to determine if you are drinking enough is to be sure that you are passing at least one and one half liters of urine per day. The color of the urine should be light yellow. If you will be traveling in a hot, humid climate you may need electrolyte supplements. Electrolyte loss is an emergency situation that should be taken seriously.

Colostomy

A person with a colostomy (especially on the left side in the descending colon), as a rule, may eat everything, although he or she should be aware of which foods cause more gas or odor. If you irrigate your colostomy you may need to make a few adjustments such as:

- ✔ Allow more time than usual for the procedure since you may need to improvise.
- ✔ Only use water that is safe to drink.
- ✔ It may be a little tricky to heat bottled water to a safe and comfortable temperature. You should bring a portable heater with a universal electrical adapter that fits the local current and outlets.
- ✔ You will need a hanger or hook to hang your water bag in different bathrooms.
- ✔ The sleeve for the returning water should be disposable so you will not need to clean one if time is limited.
- ✔ If the hour you are irrigating is much earlier than your usual time you may experience some difficulty in either introducing water or evacuating it. You may want to change to a different pattern before starting a trip. Major changes to your schedule may need a three-to-four-week adjustment period and should be done with guidance from

your ET nurse.

Continent Ileostomy

The same rules about fluid intake apply to continent ileostomy as for a person with a regular (Brook's) ileostomy. Foods containing a lot of roughage such as mushrooms, celery or corn should be avoided as they may block the catheter used to empty the pouch. It is essential to carry a travel card or alert bracelet explaining what kind of stoma you have, the need to empty it by means of a catheter and the addresses and telephone numbers of ET nurses or ostomy organizations, should any emergency occur. For irrigating the pouch and cleaning the catheter and syringe, use only water that is safe to drink.

Urostomy

Keep a leg bag handy for long trips. Try it before departing from home so that you will be able to obtain a suitable connector to your regular bag and have time to get used to it. In order to avoid any possible contamination of your urinary system it is recommended that you acidify your urine by taking Vitamin C. Consult your doctor and take the brand and dosage he or she recommends.

When Traveling in Hot Weather

Use common sense. Drink a lot of fluids, especially water (remember the safety rules). In places where water is not safe to drink, use only bottled water without ice cubes. Wear a hat, don't stay in the sun, use protective lotion and wear loose, cool clothing.

CHAPTER SEVEN

Exercise and Travel

Kerry McGinn

Three people who just happen to have ostomies anticipate their upcoming travels: Joanie, avid exerciser, crams her backpack with bicycle gear, hiking boots, running shoes and ostomy supplies as she prepares for her biking/ hiking/swimming vacation in a Canadian wilderness area. She barely broke stride when she underwent ileostomy surgery two years ago. Now she gets up early most mornings for a several-mile run before work and then puts in a couple of hours at the gym after work. Just thinking about her exercise routine—let alone doing it—strikes terror into most of us less-committed athletes.

At the opposite extreme, Carl, dedicated couch potato, has settled on a daily calisthenics routine that suits him just fine. He emerges from his recliner, trudges to his car in the driveway, drives the two blocks to the neighborhood convenience store for a large bag of corn chips and a couple cans of beer, and then returns to his recliner where he energetically exercises his thumb on the TV remote control. His wife urges him to be more active and his doctor has tried to scare him into some exercise, but Carl considers his urinary diversion four years ago the perfect excuse to avoid something he doesn't want to do anyway. "I'm too tired to exercise," he explains.

However, now his wife has finally convinced him to escape the winter doldrums with a Caribbean cruise. Even as he peruses the cruise brochure, savoring the thought of meals at all hours and a chocolate on his pillow at night, he shudders at the thought of how his expanding girth will look in cruise clothes.

Barbara, somewhere in the middle of the exercise spectrum, excitedly packs for her first trip to a United Ostomy Association conference halfway across the country. When she underwent colostomy surgery eight years ago, she thought her traveling and exercising days were over, but she has rediscovered both, and now delights in walking briskly two or three miles a few times a week with a friend. "Good for the body and the soul," is how she puts it. She knows that the conference will include plenty of sitting, along with new friends, but she has scouted out the Fun

Run/Walk one day, checked out the map and a tour book for nearby walking opportunities, and learned that her hotel has a swimming pool. She's prepared!

Our bodies are meant to move. A reasonable amount of exercise helps the heart and lungs to function the way they should, the muscles to remain strong and the bones sturdy, and the digestive tract to work smoothly. Exercise remains one of the best—and cheapest—antidotes we have for stress and depression. Surprisingly enough, exercise, properly done, increases our energy rather than depleting it. When we exercise, we eat better, sleep better, and just feel better. And exercise is fun, as long as we choose something that appeals to us. (If I hate jogging, but love to tango, then jogging is the wrong exercise for me, and dancing is just right.)

Effective exercise focuses on four areas that help us stay healthy: endurance, strength, balance, and flexibility. Aerobic (or oxygen-using) exercise, the kind of activity that makes our hearts beat faster and our breathing to deepen for an extended period, increases our endurance and thus is often called endurance exercise. By helping our lungs, heart and blood vessels to stay healthy, endurance exercises improve our stamina, our ability to perform tasks. Strength, or muscle-building, exercises, such as weight training (as simple as carrying luggage) build muscles and stronger bones, while increasing metabolism that, in turn, decreases weight. Lower body strength exercises often also improve balance, especially when we do them while holding on to a table or chair with only one hand, or a finger, or not holding on at all. Finally, we increase flexibility with stretching exercises, in which we slowly stretch into a position, hold it for 10 to 30 seconds, and then relax.

Some ostomates discovered long ago, whether before or after ostomy surgery, that exercise works wonders for them. When they travel, they may use exercise to get from one place to another, perhaps backpacking, walking or bicycling.

Barry, for instance, with an ileostomy for more than 10 years, rides his bike 14 miles a day, just back and forth to work. It's no surprise that he and his wife Ann, an equally ardent cyclist, choose vacations where they can continue "their" sport. On weekends, they often cycle from home to some scenic destination 50 miles away. For vacations, they started with organized bicycle tours through their state. By now, they've ridden through parts of New England, Eastern Canada, England and France.

Barry makes it a practice to change his pouch soon before leaving on a bike tour, but long enough before so that the seal is well set. With a few missteps along the way, Barry has learned that, as far as his ostomy is concerned, he needs very little:

1) Enough (and a few extra) supplies, which he keeps in his bike bag or in a fanny pack; this includes cleansing wipes and squares of aluminum foil for pouch disposal in case of a leak.

2) A pouch that will stay on securely despite vigorous activity and sweat (he adds a cummerbund to his regular pouch and skin barrier during cycling).

3) Someplace to empty his pouch regularly (similar to Ann's needs for toileting).

4) Replacement for fluids and salts he loses through his ileostomy during exercise; while Ann carries bottled water, Barry often carries bottled sports drinks.

Other people with ostomies take pains to vacation where they will have access to some kind of exercise they enjoy, perhaps swimming in the ocean or the motel swimming pool, dropping in at a local gym or dance studio at the travel destination, or simply walking briskly at a nature site or around a new city. They relish the combination of a familiar activity with an unfamiliar place. They know what supplies they need and how their body reacts to this kind of exercise, which simplifies the travel adjustment.

As she's grown a little older, Sheila—tireless exerciser and traveler—has changed her preferred activities. In her late 30s, years after ileostomy surgery, she slowly began jogging and, at about 50, eventually ran a marathon. Now in her 60s, and living in a much colder climate, she still runs sometimes, but has become an avid fast dancer, something she can do indoors when the weather outside is sub-zero. Wherever she travels, she finds a place where she can dance for hours. "It's so much fun! I know it keeps my heart and lungs and bones strong, and it means I can eat without worrying quite so much about getting fat—but that's only part of why I do it. Mostly it's just because it's fun and makes me feel good."

And finally, there are those who want to try a new activity to go along with their other fresh travel experiences. Perhaps, generally physically fit already, they yearn for an exercise characteristic of the place they're going, such as snorkeling or scuba diving in Hawaii or horseback riding in Montana. Or, like couch potato Carl, they might be thinking about becoming a bit more active, and the trip seems a perfect carrot on a string.

What might motivate Carl to walk a little, or swim a little—and how can he do it safely? In Carl's case, some of what his wife and doctor have been telling him has slowly been percolating in his brain. Maybe his cancer isn't a death sentence; maybe there's some life in the old guy yet. His doctor says that Carl is cancer free, but courting heart problems and diabetes with his extra weight and lack of fitness.

It wasn't more than 40 years ago that he was on the junior varsity high school football team. He really was in shape then, and he sure felt better. And as for his belly—he has to admit that the larger pant sizes have more to do with extra pounds than with an ostomy pouch. Plus, at work, there are all these younger, slimmer guys.

This combination of good memories and hope for a slimmer, healthier body persuaded Carl into increasing his activity level. Fortunately, this takes place several weeks before the cruise, which gives Carl time to check with his doctor about safe exercise for him and to build up slowly before cruise day. He intelligently decides to start out with gentle stretching, warm-up, about 10 minutes of walking, and then a cool-down for the first week—rather than the wild football game with his children that he first intended. This saves him the kind of injuries (or a heart attack) that might sideline his exercise program. By the time the cruise ship embarks, Carl is up to 20 minutes of brisk walking five times a week, feels much more energetic, and looks quite respectable in his swim trunks.

On the cruise, he overdoes it at least once, leading to some mildly sore muscles the next day, but generally enjoys walking a few laps around the deck each day, swimming slowly, and exploring the land destinations. He feels like a new man, and plans to continue regular exercise at home. (His wife is thrilled!) Before the cruise, he had a few questions about a secure pouch—during swimming for instance—that were answered by his enterostomal therapist and a friend in the United Ostomy Association. He decided to use a nylon belt with his pouch and he wore a pair of jockey shorts under his boxer-style swim trunks.

Research shows that even increases in general physical activity, which is any body movement that burns calories, produce some of the same benefits that vigorous exercise, physical activity with a planned format does. Physical activity includes such movements as those in housework, gardening, or climbing the stairs at home. During travel, walking around a tour site, climbing stairs, carrying luggage, stretching to put objects in over-head airplane luggage bins and all sorts of other physical activities increase general fitness. Growing more physically active starts with becoming more aware of all the opportunities out there.

Most ostomates who travel have at least basic ostomy care skills. Taking to the road simply means polishing those skills a bit to take into consideration being away from home and perhaps doing some unfamiliar activities. A few general suggestions, some applicable to anyone and others especially for those with ostomies:

Don't make sudden major changes in your exercise level while traveling.

The best advice here is to become reasonably fit before traveling. What "reasonably fit" means depends on your own situation, of course, but the goal is for you to be able to do comfortably at home the kind and amount of exercise that you plan to do on the trip. Most people, even without preparation, can manage a level, one-mile nature walk, but if you plan to do much more than that, work on your fitness beforehand.

Mary Ann, never an athlete before, discovered the joys of exercise during a three-week car-camping trip with her husband through Oregon, Washington and Western Canada. "First, there was this short nature trail at the state beach in Oregon. It was so beautiful—and it felt so good to move—that I was hooked!" explains Mary Ann, a 55-year-old woman with a colostomy. "I dragged my husband along on the next nature trail, a little longer, and by the end of the trip, I was quite comfortable walking briskly about two miles. My body and soul both felt alive. I've kept walking ever since."

(An excellent free resource for the person over 50—with or without an ostomy—who wants to begin or get back into exercise is the 100-page booklet, *Exercise: A Guide from the National Institute on Aging*. Available for the asking, by telephone at 800-222-2225 or on the Internet at www.nih.gov/nia. The booklet covers motivation, specific exercises, safety, benefits, self-testing and other areas.)

Stay active even when you can't exercise.
Many travels involve long periods on a plane, train, bus or in a car. This kind of enforced inactivity is no good for human beings (swollen feet, fatigue, constipation and soreness are common effects, with blood clots a serious possible problem). Getting up and walking around, when possible, helps; chair exercises at least every hour when you're awake, including tightening the leg muscles and moving the legs and shoulders, keep the body moving somewhat.

For Joe, a 72-year-old man with a colostomy, this meant making changes in what he did during a one-week bus tour in England. During a similar earlier trip, he had stayed on the bus all day listening to the tour guide. He found that he felt logy and sluggish most of the time, and constipation gave him trouble. This time, more aware of the benefits of physical activity, he discovered that he felt much better if he got out at each stop and walked around, even a half block or so. He walked up a flight of stairs rather than taking the elevator, and carried his own purchases back to the bus rather than having them brought for him. Looking for opportunities to be active became a game for him, an enjoyable part of the travel experience. He also found that the more he did, the more he wanted to do.

Be aware of changes in environment from back home and make allowances for them.
The most common changes are weather, altitude and air quality. Weather that is much warmer or colder makes a difference in what kind of exercise and how much you can do. Sometimes, if you've gone from a moderate climate to a blazingly hot one, you can exercise early in the morning or fairly late in the day and not notice much of a difference from home, but sometimes it makes sense to change the type and amount of exercise (from running to swimming, for instance). A hotter climate also means greater needs for replacing fluids and electrolytes, especially for people with ileostomies who tend to lose fluids and salts faster than those with other ostomies.

On the other hand, if you've traveled from sweltering summer or freezing winter to a moderate climate, you may be tempted to overdo—with the result of badly strained muscles. Anyone who travels to a much higher altitude, perhaps 5000 to 7000 feet higher than the familiar altitude, or to an area with significantly poorer air quality, may discover that the same amount of exercise that feels good at home is now exhausting.

Jerry, a 32-year old runner with an ileostomy who lives on the Northern California coast, where the temperature rarely

reaches 75 degrees, found running in Minneapolis in July a quite different experience.
Taking his usual 10-mile run, he needed far
more sports drink, and he found that the
extra sweat loosened his pouch. He timed his
next run for early in the morning and he
added a belt for his pouch for extra security.

Be sensible about personal safety.
Get information beforehand about the safety
of an unfamiliar area, especially if you plan
to walk or jog, and go with a friend. Keep a
map of the area with you so you won't get
lost—and always carry with you an identification card with a local phone number plus
coins or a phone card. While it is unlikely you
will need to use a personal safety device, it
makes sense to find out if there are legal
restrictions on these devices; for instance,
loud whistles should be allowed everywhere,
but sprays are illegal in many locations.

   Jenny, for instance, planned to start her
customary three-mile walk at the hotel and
see some of the city along the way. To her dis-
may, she learned from the hotel concierge
that the path she planned to walk would take
her through a decidedly seedy area. She
revamped her route and talked her friend
into walking with her.

Bring adequate ostomy supplies and store them correctly.

The rule of thumb when traveling is to bring twice as much as you think you'll need—and that may increase if you plan to exercise vigorously. Storage for take-along supplies becomes a problem if you'll be exercising in the sun and carrying some supplies with you, such as on a long run or bike ride. A fanny pack may be cooler than a backpack; a small, insulated container—available at sports or travel stores—may help.

Essential non-ostomy supplies include comfortable exercise shoes and a small stash of foot care products, such as a small sheet each of moleskin and foam and scissors to cut them. A first aid kit geared to the exerciser should contain an ACE wrap compression bandage and an instant ice pack as well as the usual Band-Aids and first aid cream. If they can tolerate this kind of medicine, many people tuck in a few non-steroidal anti-inflammatory pills (NSAIDS) such as ibuprofen or Naproxen to help reduce muscle swelling and pain if they occur.

An ostomy is no bar to exercise. Whatever the type of exercise, someone with an ostomy, somewhere, does it and relishes it. Travel simply adds to the fun, as long as the person with an ostomy plans ahead a bit and realizes that a surprise or two may be part of this memorable experience in fresh surroundings. Enjoy!

CHAPTER EIGHT

Modes of Travel

"Kathy"
Ileostomy, United States

My main travel experiences are by boat on the Hudson River and Long Island Sound. My husband and I have a 27-foot Sea Ray and have spent many enjoyable long weekends aboard the boat with our daughter. Having an ileostomy done in October 1997 was the best thing that ever happened to us. Traveling by boat was possible, if not a little confining. The "head" on a 27-foot boat is not big but it is functional.

Kathy Foley-Bolch
...On Modes of Travel

Since the beginning of time people have had to get from one point to the other by whatever means possible. This is a brief summation of some of the ways those of us with ostomies can accomplish this.

Walking

As crazy as it sounds, walking is one of the most common ways to get from Point A to Point B. It's also one of the easiest, and needs the least preparation for us to get started. Comfortable shoes, a bottle of water, a freshly emptied appliance, and comfortable clothes that help to hold your pouch in place are all that is needed. With this you can go out to the mailbox, or across the country if that is what you desire. It also helps you to stay healthy by providing aerobic exercise, and is an important deterrent for diseases like osteoporosis, which many of us are more prone to due to the medications we have been on for our diseases.

Driving

Once again, an activity so common that most of us do not even think of it as travel, but it is. The thing to remember with driving is if you're going to be in the vehicle for a long period of time, plan plenty of rest stops in order to avoid fatigue and stiffness, and again, bring your water. I've found this helps to insure the frequent rest stops! And if your traveling companion is like mine and gets in the vehicle and goes, make sure you lay the ground rules before setting out.

Many people are afraid of using a seat belt because they fear harm to their stomas. A clothespin works wonders in adjusting the seat belt to the most comfortable position for you.

When we go for long trips, I always keep a spare appliance in my purse, and one in a waterproof bag in the cooler, just in case. You don't want to put them in the trunk or the glove box, because the properties of an appliance degrade so quickly in temperature extremes. These are some tricks that I learned while driving a tractor-trailer and a motor home across the country.

Airplanes

This has been discussed in detail in other sections of the book, but my tips include: comfortable clothes, lots of water, and sitting in the emergency exit aisle if at all possible, because it has the most room to stretch your legs. Of course, there's some responsibility to sitting here, and if you aren't willing or able to help other passengers should the need arise, this isn't the seat for you.

My pouch has never blown up or expanded due to altitude, and I don't even try to sit near the restrooms. I find there is too much activity there from other passengers, and it is quieter other places. My biggest problem is the gas that inevitably occurs when I sleep, and a long plane ride could find me waking up with the Hindenburg on my belly, so a long shirt is important to conceal this lopsided problem. I also have my pilot's license, and small planes offer no challenges that are different from a car ride.

Trains

I haven't ridden on a train since my surgery (actually, I don't think I've ever ridden on a train!) so I can only suggest that you check the accommodations prior to your trip. I'm sure they are similar to the airlines. I have ridden on a subway, and the challenge to that in the Boston area is to avoid being inadvertently elbowed or jostled around.

Motorcycles

Prior to my surgery, both my husband and I rode motorcycles, and I was sure this was something that would have to be forgotten forever. It took me awhile to get back to it, and I was cautious when I did start back. The thing that made me most comfortable in riding was leather. When I decided to get back to it, we went to a motorcycle show, and I was able to find a long leather pullover shirt. That gave me my freedom back, because it covered my stoma, and was comfortable. I've since gotten a long leather car stadium jacket that has great pockets for holding an extra appliance, and anything else I need for a day trip.

I also have adapted a shin protector that is used for bike racing to slip down into my jeans, but I have found that to be a little restrictive, although it originally gave me the confidence to ride again. As you can see, there really is no limit to what you can do. Anything you could do before, you can do now. Just be smart about new experiences, and get out there and go!

Travel With an Ostomy? Piece of Cake!
Janie Graziani

In the first place, it was way too cold to be outside. Thirty below was specifically designed so people would have a perfect excuse to stay snuggled under the eiderdown or in front of a roaring fire. But there she was, in a "sled" chair (as opposed to one with wheels), being pushed along by her companion. I supposed that even people who can't hop from foot to foot to keep the blood from freezing in their veins had a right to go outside even when they had the ideal reason to stay in. I was curious, though, what she was doing at the kennels where the sled dogs were kept. I was there because I was about to get my very first dog-mushing lesson. (What was I thinking? I don't even like the cold.)

So I watched. Her companion pushed the chair right beside a sled with a team already hitched. Easy as you please, she picked herself up with upper body strength and plopped down on a pile of reindeer furs on the sled, pulling one of them over her and tucking it around her legs for warmth. (If you can't feel anything, how do you know if you are getting frostbite? I thought absently.)

Even though I was trying not to stare, what happened next made me stop in my tracks, mouth gaping. He handed her the reins. With a soft whistle, the 14-dog team set out for the trail, taking the woman and her friend down a small hill and into the woods where they disappeared from view.

Within moments, my opinion of people with disabilities rose a hundredfold. Anyone who can mush a dogsled team, even pick themselves up like that and move, can do anything they want as far as I'm concerned. And traveling? Piece of cake.

By the way, my first attempt at driving the team was not nearly as successful: I ended up flat on my face in the snow and the dogs were 30 yards away before they stopped. Here are few tips I've picked up after many years of travel and working with AAA that may make your travel a little easier.

The two most important people you can talk to prior to taking a trip are your doctor and a travel agent. Talk with the doctor first, although you may go back to him or her several times in the vacation planning stages.

Your physician can tell you whether or not you should travel, whether any modes of transportation or destinations should be avoided and what effect, if any, your planned activities may have on you because of your condition.

Use a travel agent. Planning a vacation is an investment in time and money. Working with a travel agent can make the planning easier and save you some time. Also, they have access to a plethora of information that would take forever for a layman to go through. For the amount of work they can do, travel agents are one of the best travel bargains around.

Make sure the travel agent knows what your specific needs are. If a door needs to be opened with a closed fist, or doors need to be a certain width, tell the travel agent. When making reservations for hotels, tours, theaters, restaurants or other entertainment make sure the person taking your order understands your special needs. For instance, motor coaches usually have a restroom in them, but if you are unsure, ask.

When packing, put all essential items such as medicines, passport, toiletries, a change of clothing and any other supplies you need in a carry-on bag and keep it with you at all times. Always keep prescription medication in its original bottle or packaging; it is easier to explain at customs and if you need a refill, the prescription is right on the bottle. If possible, get copies of your prescriptions from your doctor to take with you. If your medicine gets lost or stolen it will be easier to replace, and you will already have your doctor's name, address and phone number with you. Also, get prescriptions to last throughout the trip and a few days more, especially if you are leaving the country.

If you are planning to rent a car, let the rental agency know whether you will need a temporary handicapped-parking permit. If they can't get one for you, at least they will know how you can get one. And make sure you get a car that can hold your wheelchair if you have one.

Trains throughout Europe and Canada are usually spacious (as far as trains go), clean, and convenient. But if you feel the least bit uncomfortable about taking one, explain your concerns to your travel agent or a supervisor at the ticketing agency. They may be able to allay your fears or suggest alternative transportation.

Airlines are one of the best reasons to use a travel agent: they already know the airlines' rules concerning special equipment such as oxygen and wheelchairs. A travel agent will also make sure that the airline is aware of your special needs, if any, before you arrive at the airport.

When flying, arrive at the airport in

plenty of time to check in and get a boarding pass. Terrorist incidents have made it impossible for travel agents to issue boarding passes so you need to check in to get one. You will also be able to get boarding passes for the entire trip.

The second-most important thing you can for yourself is to buy trip insurance. For a few hundred dollars, you can insure your travel investment for such things as medical emergencies (whether before you leave or while you are traveling), financial default by a travel vendor, strikes or natural disasters that require a travel carrier to halt services, terrorist incidents, some traffic accidents, and even lost or stolen baggage. Some policies offer legal help as well as medical assistance. It is another great travel value for an excellent policy.

There is plenty of assistance out there for those who want to travel but feel reluctant to because of a disability. As I said before, there is no reason why those who have disabilities should stay home when they could be out enjoying a crisp, cold morning of dog mushing.

CHAPTER NINE

Toileting

Carol Norris

Lying in the hospital with our new stomas, most of us who were patients in the 1960s learned not to be impatient. Little information was available; the United Ostomy Association appeared during the sixties as a source of information, but no enterostomal therapist yet existed. Lucky me, before my three-month summer hospital stay ended, a doctor told me about the new *Ostomy Quarterly* magazine. Information was still scant. For instance, was there any evidence that fulminating-ulcerative colitis ileostomates like me could bear children? Ten years later I helped write a UOA booklet on pregnancy with an ostomy, although I, myself—and not because of the ostomy—chose career over motherhood. I still have no regrets, having by now become a... well, a lil' old grand-teacher. My career, however, not to mention travel was in doubt during the summer of 1963. Concerned friends warned me never to expect to teach again. I surprised them. By October of that year, one month after my second—and still final surgery—I was again teaching college English.

In the year following surgery, I tented across the USA and Canada with my botanist husband. We later traveled across Europe and visited Australia. I started to run when my husband did (at the age of 38), I managed almost 20 years after my surgery, to finish, albeit very slowly, the Helsinki City Marathon in Finland. I strongly recommend long, slow running (I still jog a mile or two and do vigorous Finnish dancing—both weekly—not weakly), and ostomates among runners do have toileting advantages. While other joggers or marathoners are wasting precious minutes in toilets along the route or having to dash into the bushes with diarrhea, an ostomate can wait and conserve. I lasted out my race with only one two minute toilet stop during my five and a half hours, and actually out-ran six people—plus the 50 who never finished at all.

I actually begin this saga on travel—toileting with tenting because any ostomate who can survive in a tent in a foreign land gains confidence in her toileting flexibility and thus in her normality. The main question is pouch emptying and changing, when one prefers not to compete for the path to the toilet with five-foot monitor lizards or leaping kangaroos. A quarter-century later, I chose, this summer not to share the path with mosquitoes or with Homo sapiens of the drunken teenage variety.

Ideally, when tenting you will travel with your own portable chemical toilet. If none is available, then choose appliances that are disposable. (Soak reusable pouches in a sealed refrigerator-type bowl or box.) But one need not even use disposable pouches. In tents and cars I emptied and changed the little basic black rubber pouches that I wore until the Finnish health care system insisted that I go modern in 1988 with two-piece pouches.

If you are camping without a chemical toilet, you can create your own. Find either a large jar (such as one for pickles or coffee), with a secure screw-on lid with several circles of threads. My favorite, however, is a squat plastic bucket of almost a quart capacity; it has a wide mouth, wire loop handle and a secure snap down lid. I recommend taking along a full set of ostomy supplies plus the following: a large jug of water, opaque plastic bags of various sizes, a box of tissues (when inverted the box makes a tiny table), a roll of toilet paper/paper towels, moist wipes, perhaps some aluminum foil and a trustworthy flashlight that can stand up on its own. With all these supplies, one can not only easily empty a pouch but can even change it. With a hook and a tent that will support a water container, or with a tripod or helpful friend one can even irrigate a colostomy. Having a helpful companion to focus the flashlight is also welcome. And don't forget your eyeglasses! It is, of course, also possible to urinate in the container, but don't over estimate your—or its—holding capacity. Then take the container to the campground or a gas station toilet in the morning. If a flush toilet is available, empty the container, flush, then flush again and rinse the container under the clean flush water as it enters. If you first line the container with a plastic bag, you will have a disposable container to empty or tie shut and place in a receptacle. In wilder conditions, dig a hole—not, remember, near any river or lake—and bury the contents or the plastic bag. You will, of course, need to bring a small shovel or trowel with you.

For outdoor latrines and for some rustic indoor toilets (such as those found at some US highway rest stops), light, paper and odor can be problematic. Remember to take a standup-type flashlight with you, even in the daytime. Once the door is closed, some toilet stalls become quite dark, making it difficult to do accurate aiming or rinsing or swabbing of a pouch opening. I have hung a cube shaped flashlight from a door latch, clamped it between my knees, and even hung it from my neck on a cord in order to provide adequate light for my activities.

Always bring your own toilet paper. Do not be defeated by foreign or domestic public toilets lacking in towels or toilet tissue. Check the supply before you commit yourself to a stall. Always take a few extra napkins from restaurants to supplement a constant tissue supply in your purse or pocket. This is a wise idea for everyone, not just ostomates. Moist-wipes come in handy as well. I spent decades carefully folding pieces of toilet paper into swabs to wipe the inside of the pouch opening either after a rinse or instead of rinsing. Finally, years after "going disposable" I reread Mullen and McGinn's *The Ostomy Book*[9] and discovered that I can turn back the mouth of my thin plastic pouch into a cuff; now I need not wipe the opening after emptying, but just turn the cuff down again. Live and learn.

To tell the truth, campers and hikers with ostomies have two toileting advantages over non-ostomates. First, we can wait far longer for a toilet opportunity, and second, out of doors, we can merely kneel, dig a hole and empty, without undressing any portion of ourselves. Mosquitoes do not have the opportunity to attack an exposed backside, or at least they lack an extended opportunity. Ostomates enjoy the same advantage when it comes to seeking a pit stop on the highway. If we supply ourselves with the sort of large lidded jar or other vessel useful in a tent, we can fill it in a car. We merely flip the pouch end out

[9] Barbara Dorr Mullen and Kerry Anne McGinn, *The Ostomy Book: Living Comfortably with Colostomies, Ileostomies, and Urostomies* (Bull Pub. Co., 1992).

of our underclothes, or out through front-opening pants and use our upper clothing to shield our actions from passersby. A coffee jar is most efficient, clamped between the knees and out of sight. Store this well-used container in an opaque plastic bag until the next restroom. For travel, I recommend front opening slacks for women and a loose shirt worn outside the pants for everyone. I have even changed an appliance in a car, first draping a towel over the nearest windows and locking all the doors.

Perhaps this is the place to mention our own odor production. Our first line of defense against offending, in a tent, car or other public place is external. Take along a deodorant or odor particle precipitator to apply to a piece of tissue and put into your underclothes. You can also place liquid or solid products in the pouch (aspirin is a No-No because it will cause your stoma to bleed; the alcohol in some mouthwashes will attack plastics), or take them orally. Read the ostomy literature or ask a knowledgeable pharmacist. Some people carry matches with them; strike a match as soon as possible after emptying, move the flame around and above you to burn up the invisible gases you have produced. The scent of the match smoke serves to cover odors as well. My best test of odor control occurred when I drove from Germany to Norway to Britain with a girl-friend, often sleeping in the back of a Volkswagen bus, vintage 1967. The space for us and our sleeping bags extended to about the interior space of ... let's say three coffins wide by two coffins in height. I had sewn curtains for the windows all around. For nighttime venting problems, I used a drop of an external odor killer on a tissue placed near my hip. My companion had, however, always known about my ileostomy.

While studying in London that summer, I decided to be a secret ostomate for once, just for the weekend I traveled with another student to Wales, sleeping in the VW. If one can sleep two in a VW bus, one can be an anonymous ostomate anytime, anywhere. On Monday, the news that I had an ileostomy truly surprised her. Why tell? Because even nowadays, even with the youngest Bush brother openly an ileostomate and Barbara Barrie[10] writing about her colostomy, ignorance exists. Normal life with an ostomy is still essential for us to reveal, so that no one because of misinformation or no information will refuse life-saving surgery.

Back to public toilets. In such toilets, ostomates—some of whom need sufficient time to empty two bladders—should be doubly careful to latch all doors securely. Twice last summer I found myself being careless about latching the doors of single-user restrooms in restaurants. Within the space of ten hours, in two countries, I left doors only semi-locked. Both times an innocent woman

---

[10] Barbara Barrie, *Second Act: Life After Colostomy and Other Adventures* (Scribner, 1997).

yanked open the door and both times I was seated and my pouch was clipless.

Toilet doors or stall doors without any locks or latches appall me. One must sit on the seat in order to hook a toe under the door, and one might prefer a squat. I have seen an *Ostomy Quarterly* advertisement for a closing device resembling two large buttons on a loop of cord; mail order miscellany companies sell similar devices for securing doors. Some men's toilets are without doors at all. I hear that male ostomates then use the toilet while sitting or standing facing the wall. Anyone sitting facing an open door should bend well forward to shield pouch-centered activities with one's clothing. Take along a "Do Not Disturb" or "Occupied" ("Occupado" might serve in more countries) sign to hang on the door. Remember that anyone opening a door or entering a doorway will be more shocked and embarrassed than you will be—and thus will not be very observant. A nineteenth century joke involves a man who walks in on a lady in a boarding-house bathtub (toilet). The man says, if merely polite, "Excuse me, Madam." However, if he is tactful he says, "Excuse me, Sir." You can be sure that even if the intruder guesses your gender, no one will be expecting to see an ostomy pouch and thus would probably not believe his or her eyes.

Civilized toilet bowls may be equipped with a deodorant container attached just under the rim. Be watchful. If such a desirable gadget is hung toward the front of the toilet bowl, it may be endangered by an ostomate's far forward maneuvers. Out of consideration for the next user, slide such a deodorant container around to the side or rear of the toilet bowl and then return it to its original position.

Experienced ostomates also plan how, in the toilet, to avoid losing track of or even losing their pouch-clip. The clip can be secured under the elastic of an undergarment or hooked on a belt-loop; it can be placed on or hooked into the toilet paper holder (or as one clever man suggested, at the beach it can be inserted between bare toes). Just remember how easily a lightweight clip can fling itself merrily down any toilet bowl. Keep extra pouch closures in every imaginable place from purse to pocket, and at all times. If you manage to leave a toilet clipless, who sells rubber bands? What is the word for rubber band in a foreign language? In general, to avoid leaving anything behind in a strange toilet, hang or set your possessions directly in the path to the door. To defeat the purse, jacket, beads, tie or anything else that is dangling in your workspace keep with you one or two snap clothespins and pin everything back. If you are wearing a top garment that buttons down the front, unbutton it, pull each side behind you and refasten it behind your back. I sometimes wear a front buttoning jacket or sweater into the toilet to button behind me in that fashion—unfashionable as that may look. Push or roll up your sleeves as well.

Some toilets away from home offer a challenge, most commonly chemical toilets on buses, trains, ships and planes. The stool's exit opening may be distressingly small and far back in the bowl. Rinse water volume is limited as is space to move around. I finally discovered one solution. Don't wait to go to the toilet until it is too late to perform your activities in reverse order. First, empty the pouch right over the exit opening, whether it is of the wide-open or hinged-flap variety. This may mean standing or crouching, or sitting on the seat sidesaddle or facing backwards. Then reposition yourself and urinate—and this goes for both genders—so that you yourself furnish the first rinse. When you use the flush button, switch or lever the toilet can to the best of its own ability and complete the washout. If this does not succeed, operate the flush mechanism again and finally use a paper towel to make the toilet bowl as clean as you found it or wish you had found it.

One traveler on a Russian train could not discover how to flush the toilet because she had set her bag down on the button on the floor. I have similarly set my purse down so as to cover up the flushing mechanism on the wall. The rule is to find out how the toilet evacuates itself before you set anything down, including yourself.

British toilets of older styles feature a multitude of flushing mechanisms. The reservoir may be an overhead tank, up under a 12—foot ceiling, with a dangling chain. A lever may project from some unexpected place. I once offended a group of Scots at a *ceolich*, a traditional dance party, with an impromptu speech about us poor Yanks trying to flush toilets of mystifying construction with their frighteningly torrential blasts of flush water. "Flush and stand well back" was good advice.

We see three types of toilets. Recently, I received encouragement from women in line behind me for the women's room to use the "handicapped" toilet, since there were no other handicapped people in line. Deciding to view myself as "intestinally handicapped" for about three minutes, I went in. I noted inside that a cord with a wooden handle was dangling from the ceiling near the toilet. When I finished, thinking smugly of my many trips to Britain, I was already gripping the handle before I saw a note stuck to the cord that said, "Pull only in emergency." The toilet actually had its flush-button on top of the tank. Pulling that particular cord would have meant having to convince the museum staff that I was indeed intestinally handicapped or be judged an inconsiderate trespasser.

Don't forget that in any strange toilet, if the water pool below you is large and extends

forward, explosive splashes will occur. To prevent splashing, drop a handful of toilet paper
onto the water first and then empty the pouch
quickly above it. Someone wondered, in print,
how this operates. I would compare it with
jumping onto a raft in the sea, versus landing
in the water itself. The raft will keep the
splash minimal and the toilet paper forms a
very temporary raft. Some European toilets,
in Germany, for instance, will surprise you by
having the water pool forward with a raised
ceramic platform behind it. Author Erica
Jong commented that such toilets allow you
to seriously contemplate your solid produce.
Such study opportunities might well save lives
by leading to earlier detection of rectal cancer and inflammatory bowel diseases by their
symptoms such as bleeding. These toilets,
however, require ostomates either to use the
toilet paper raft technique described above
or to choose a different body stance while
emptying, like sitting facing the wall.

In Finland, you will meet a device that I
wager many will covet for their toilets at
home: The bidetsuihku or bidet shower. This
is a spray head close to the toilet on a hose
running either to the sink pipes or even to a
little sink in the stall itself. It may also be
attached to a faucet handle projecting from
the wall. Check first to see whether the spray
head itself has an on—off switch. If it does,
you can turn on the water, choose the temperature and then at leisure start the spray. If

not, you must position the spray head facing into the toilet bowl before you start the spray from the faucet handle. Otherwise you can be doused. Carefully control the water volume so that you can tilt the head and allow a slow, thin stream, not a spray, to enter the opening of the pouch or anything else needing a rinse. This can be challenging but is very important.

Irrigating colostomates must consider more than their water source and how it is delivered. Their irrigation water should be as pure as the water they drink. When one lives in a different country, state or province, one's intestines become accustomed to different varieties of our normally harmless, often essential intestinal flora (mainly E. coli). The close cousins of such organisms can cause diarrhea. Treatment may be as simple as drinking a bottle of Pepto-Bismol or some other product with adsorptive abilities. Before traveling, ask your pharmacist what to take with you.

Boiling water for three minutes is thought to kill most bacteria. Also sold are water sterilizing tablets to be added to water. You can add 10 drops of chlorine bleach to a quart of water and let this stand for half an hour according to *The Ostomy Book*[11] which also suggests using beer or soft drinks as a last resort. The beer or soft drinks should be de-fizzed by shaking or allowing them to stand open. The same Russian traveler who lost the train toilet flush button cleverly used

[11] Barbara Dorr Mullen and Kerry Anne McGinn, *The Ostomy Book: Living Comfortably with Colostomies, Ileostomies, and Urostomies* (Bull Pub. Co., 1992).

water boiled in the Russian's ever-present tea samovar. You can buy twice the amount of bottled water you need—from a reputable source and in sealed bottles—and carry it back to your room or tent or carry it with you on the train. I myself drink so much water that I already out-purchase any non-ostomate but no one comments. My father (a sea captain, no ostomate), did the same and labeled himself a "waterholic."

Hanging an irrigation bag is a problem, and the ostomy literature is full of designs for hooks and cords. A large S-shaped hook is always handy, but to hook anything over the top edge of most doors or stalls, you need a thin, flat L-or U-shaped device. A wire coat hanger or two is always useful to bend into many shapes to suit your needs. Take a set of metal shower-curtain loops and make a chain? Don't forget a few feet of strong cord. Most tripods are either too heavy or fragile to carry on trips. Remember all those mobile hospital IV stands? If a portable tripod is too fragile to support a reservoir, can a colostomate bring along a large bottle of water and add water gradually to the reservoir while irrigating? Or would that require the dexterity of an octopus?

A small bottle filled from your bottled water supply or from the sink tap is useful for pouch and bowl cleaning. One with a push-pull squirt cap is best. No one will stare at you if you fill a bottle at the sink before going into a stall; let them imagine you are diluting a dose of medicine or watering down your afternoon gin. I like to pack a small, unbreakable pitcher with a thin spout, like the one that dwells beside my toilet at home, and let people think I am planning to have my afternoon tea in the stall. At least have a plastic cup with you. And don't forget to always bring along soap.

Urostomates, unlike other ostomates, must take great care with their hygiene in order to avoid infection of the kidneys or ureters. Infection is usually heralded by fever, chills, pain or discolored or odorous urine. External urostomy pouches should be disposable or be carefully soaked and cleaned. As for ileostomates and colostomates, it is in the toilet that they may first notice urethritis, a major symptom of which is a sudden burning at the start and at the end of urination.

Now researchers have discovered what is in cranberries[12] that helps to prevent and even cure such urinary infections. A chemical called tannin interferes with the attachment of E. coli bacteria to the urinary tract lining. The benefit of cranberry (and to a lesser extent raspberry and blueberry) products results from far more than a slight acidification of the urine.

Regardless of the type of surgery, one can sometimes find an unfamiliar toilet that seems eager to trap a traveler, even one—a toilet and traveler, as well—with all interior

[12] J. Avorn, M. Monane, J.H. Gurwitz, R.J. Glynn, I. Choodnovskiy, L.A. Lipitz, "Reduction of Bacteriuria and Pyuria After Ingestion of Cranberry Juice," *Journal of the American Medical Association*, March 1994. For further references on the benefits of cranberries, please see Bibliography.

plumbing. I have no memories of anything daunting in Mexico in 1970 or in Fiji in 1974 or in Papua New Guinea in 1984. The only hole-in-the-floor squat toilet I found was in 1973 in Singapore, and a friend found one in 1992 in an Italian railway station. For that type what you need most is strong leg muscles. If you have sufficient disposable padding, you can kneel over a squat toilet-hole on one knee.

The worst problem I encountered was from Australia to Canada to Estonia: the two-room system of a "bathroom" containing a sink and bathtub and then perhaps far down the hall, a small "toilet" with only the toilet and no sink/water supply. This requires water carrying from the bathroom, which may well be occupied. If your bedroom has a sink, the supply problem will be lessened. In bedrooms with sinks, I usually find it easier to change my pouch in that room, I first line a trashcan with a plastic bag (nothing is handier than plastic bags, by the way, from bread wrappers to grocery and garbage bags). Confidence grows from practice dealing with pouches in a car or tent. An appliance change or irrigation done anywhere requires a small table. A chair can be imported to serve as a table. You can also invert a trashcan; this is what I usually do to create table space. Trashcans can also serve as emergency sinks for soaking equipment. Prepare everything ahead of time, of course: the new appli-

ance, a stack of paper towels or lengths of toilet paper, a vessel to pour water, water and a
disposal bag before you settle down for the
big switch.

In foreign lands, the local language most
critically interferes when you are on a hunt
for a public restroom. (Don't use that term,
unless you want to be asked: "Do you really
go there for a rest?" Ask for the toilet
instead). But be assured that the problem of
recognizing your own gender is fast being
solved. In 1978, knowing no Finnish, I was
alone on Suomenlinna fortress isle off
Helsinki faced with two outhouses bearing
the labels "N" and "M." Luckily I chose "N"
which means "Naiset" whereas "Meihet"
means men. Nowadays, tourism booms and
countries also use silhouettes of male and
female figures. I checked and found this is
true now on Suomenlinna. One can also
expect silhouettes of ... roosters and hens.
One clever US hunting club is reported to
use pictures of a setter and a pointer (dog).
The word "toilet" serves everywhere. We also
meet "M/F," "His/Hers," "Herren/Damen,"
"Gents/Ladies." I hope no one ever misspells
"Ladies" as "Laddies," "WC" means water
closet in British-influenced lands, even in
Finland where it is pronounced not "double-
u-see" but "vessa," "Loo" is common in
British speech and the British term "Lavatory" is pronounced much like the US "Labo-
ratory." In the US the words "john" and

"head" and some other ruder terms must puzzle tourists.

This little exposition on the joys and problems of toileting will end with the most daunting toilet challenge imaginable. A British grandmother actually sailed cheerfully for three days and nights in a "smallish sailing boat" through storms and gale-force winds with her grown son and two other men, none of whom knew she had an ostomy. In the "head," less than three feet on a side and without handholds, she was able to balance in a rolling boat, managing a pouch and five layers of clothing, including heavy oilskins. She even expressed sympathy for the greater problems faced by the men. Although I travel by sea as often as possible, and once took an overnight trip along the Papua New Guinea coast, sleeping on the deck of a small ferry, that British ostomate's feat is one that this sea captain's daughter never wants to even attempt.

CHAPTER TEN

Special Considerations

Julie Carr, RN and
Louisa Corazzini, BS, RN

Introduction

While you may experience change in your daily routine, your ostomy surgery should not gain control of your life. The purpose of this chapter is to discuss special considerations that you may need to take after surgery. Regular examination of the stoma and peristomal skin is very important. Choice in clothing and issues of intimacy are also prime concerns. Creative planning for travel is needed. Although some changes are required, you can enjoy many activities and lead a happy life after surgery.

Stoma Examination

You should examine your stoma regularly to ensure its visibility. Stoma is the Greek word for mouth, and the stomal color should be similar to the inside of a healthy mouth (Convatec, 1998). Initially after surgery, the stoma is swollen, but it will shrink to its true size in the first six to eight weeks (Krames, 1997). The stoma does not have nerve endings, but it does have a strong blood supply. If irritated, the stoma can bleed. Properly fitting pouches are essential to prevent problems of the stoma. There should be 1/8 inch of distance between the opening of the ostomy appliance and the stoma (Krames, 1997). A poorly fitting pouch could pinch the stoma, which could lead to laceration and bleeding. When you change your pouch, you should inspect your stoma well. The color should be beefy red, and the stoma should be moist (Erwin-Toth & Doughty, 1992). This should be done on a weekly basis to prevent any complications.

Peristomal Skin Issues

A leaking pouch is a major source of skin problems. The type of ostomy and the consistency of the urine or stool determine the amount of damage that has been caused to the peristomal skin. The length of time that the pouch is allowed to leak is also another important consideration. If the problem is not corrected, severe peristomal skin irritation can occur. This problem is called irritant dermatitis and can become very painful. Ileostomy effluent contains many pancreatic enzymes that can severely damage the skin (Convatec, 1998). Colostomy leakage varies with the location of the stoma. Sigmoid and descending ostomies have stool that is firm while the ascending and transverse colostomies can vary from a paste to a liquid-type stool (Krames, 1997). Leakage from a urostomy can lead to hyperplasia, which is the development of wart-like growths on the skin (Hampton, 1992). A properly fitting pouch is the first step to good stoma care.

Other peristomal skin issues can occur that will affect all activities. An allergic reaction to a product can cause the skin to become inflamed, to swell, and to burn. If this problem does develop, you must determine what product caused the reaction. Change your pouching system or eliminate the product that caused you harm. When these types of sensitivities develop, they often last for life (Hampton, 1992). A major question, when you have a great deal of hair around the stoma, is whether to shave the area regularly. Pulling off hair at the time of pouch removal could lead to problems, but shaving the hair off can also lead to damage. When you change your pouch, remove it gently. Irritated peristomal skin is an unpleasant complication called folliculitis (Hampton, 1992).

Fungal infections are unpleasant peristomal skin problems that are caused by excess moisture. An itchy red pimple-like rash may appear under the ostomy wafer. If this infection is not treated, it can lead to severe skin problems and affect the adherence of the ostomy wafer. It is important to prevent excess moisture under the appliance. Leakage and perspiration are the prime suspects if this problem develops. Prevention consists of: 1. A properly fitting pouch, 2. A pouch cover, 3. Changing your appliance in warm weather. If the problem develops, usually an anti-fungal powder will be required to treat the affected area (Hampton, 1992).

Adhesive build-up and the use of soaps can lead to skin problems. When you change your pouch, cleanse away all adhesive residue. This can be done with warm water and a little elbow grease. There are commercial adhesive removers, but often insurers do not pay for them. If your use these products, you must rinse them off thoroughly. The use of soaps can lead to a build-up of film on the skin. This can create problems for pouch adherence. The best rule of thumb is to use the least number of products as possible on your skin.

Clothing and Intimacy

There is no need to change your wardrobe since you have had ostomy surgery. Modern pouches lie flat against the body, and no one can guess that you have an ostomy from the front or side view of you. Only those that you choose to tell will know about your pouch. If you like tight clothes, wear them. Shorts, stretch pants and all the latest fashions are acceptable. You are not limited to loose jumpers or extra large pants. Your pouch may be placed inside or outside your underwear. Men can wear boxers or briefs. If your stoma is near your waist, avoid belts and waistbands that might rub against the stoma.

Personal intimacy is a basic human need. Ostomy surgery does not take away the need for love or the touch of another. Your stoma is a part of you, not the total you. If you are beginning a new relationship, tell the other person about the ostomy when appropriate to you. Talk to your partner about this issue before your relationship becomes intimate (Krames, 1997). Sexual relations do not hurt the stoma in any way, although some males have performance side effects from urostomy and lower bowel surgery. If you are in an established relationship, relax! There are many ways to express your love without actually making love. Hugging, kissing, and just talking can be fun. When you are able to be intimate with your partner, empty your pouch before sex. A small pouch, pouch cover, or opaque pouch might make you feel comfortable. Special nightgowns, underwear, or lotions may enhance your experience, but always remember your partner loves you. The stoma has not made changes to the wonderful person that you are.

Travel and Leisure

There are no restrictions on travel after ostomy surgery. A little planning will prevent any complications that could occur. Remember your supplies, and put them in your carry-on luggage. Do not put your supplies in hot, confined places such as trunks of cars—and carry a card with the code numbers of the manufacturer. If you are traveling outside the United States, an ostomy supply store of a hospital may be able to help you. When you are traveling in under-developed areas, you must make sure that you have adequate supplies. Bring a supply of resealable plastic bags-which come in handy in many situations. Go camping and enjoy. In fact, this is a time when you have the advantage since others may find it difficult without a proper commode. Watch your diet and avoid ice and tap water, unpeeled fruits and vegetables in foreign countries (Krames, 1997). Enjoy the trip and see all the sights.

The most important consideration is

that you accept yourself. The stoma has not changed the special person that you are. Do whatever you want with your leisure time. The only restrictions are contact sports without adaptive equipment to protect the stoma, and heavy lifting (Krames, 1997). Treasure your leisure time and have fun. Your stoma has improved your health, but it has not altered the all-important you.

CHAPTER ELEVEN

When to Take Action

Julie Carr, RN

Early recognition of potential problems can prevent complications both at home and away. The purpose of this chapter is to address some of the possible situations, such as blockages or dehydration for the ileostomate, constipation for the person with a colostomy, and urinary tract infections and stone formation for urostomates. All of the above could affect your well-being-and early recognition can prevent an emergency situation.

Stomal Complications

Prolapse and Hernia
Prolapse and hernia are two potentially serious complications of the stoma. Prolapse

is a falling away of the stoma from the abdominal wall. It can be caused from an abdominal opening that is too large and allows the intestine to travel downward, and can frequently occur with a transverse loop stoma. A hernia results from placing the stoma in a weak area of the abdominal wall outside the abdominal muscle. If stomal function is not impaired, either situation should just be monitored. If the blood supply to the stoma is affected by prolapse, or function is impaired by hernia, a visit to a surgeon is required. (Hampton, 1992).

Stenosis

This problem consists of a narrowing of the opening of the stoma. It is caused by
1. Poor stoma location,
2. Inadequate blood supply to the stoma, or
3. Stomal retraction (Cellestin, 1986). It may be difficult for the stool or urine to travel through the opening of the stoma, and there is a potential for a partial obstruction.

For ileostomies, look for the following signs:
1. Abdominal cramps,
2. Nausea,
3. Diarrhea,
4. Projectile stool.

Those with colostomies could experience
1. Abdominal cramps,
2. Explosive stool,
3. Excessive gas, or
4. Episodes of diarrhea.

Urinary stomas react in some of the following ways:
1. Urinary tract infections,
2. Projectile urine,
3. Decreased urine output,
4. Pain on the side of the body (Hampton, 1992).

As you can imagine, it is important to seek medical attention if you are experiencing these problems, as ignoring them can lead to serious complications.

Additionally, as you might realize, these problems are not as likely to first occur on your trip, but it's good to know how to handle things as they arise.

Ileostomy Concerns

People with ileostomies have two major issues that can lead to serious complications: food blockage and fluid imbalance.

Food blockages are caused when high fiber foods block the opening of the stoma (Bryant, Doughty & Fitzgerald, 1992). Exam-

ples of foods that can cause problems are
1. Apple skins,
2. Celery,
3. Chinese vegetables,
4. Popcorn,
5. Raisins,
6. Potato skins,
7. Dried fruits, or
8. Meat with casings.

Chewing your food well and drinking plenty of fluids will help prevent problems. Reintroducing any of these foods back into your diet slowly will also help (Convatec, 1998).

The signs of a complete or partial blockage of the ileum are important to know. Partial obstruction may have the following symptoms:
1. Abdominal pain,
2. Watery output with foul odor, or
3. Abdominal and stomal swelling.

Complete obstruction can have these signs:
1. Absence of output,
2. Severe cramping, or
3. Abdominal and stomal pain.

If you have an ileostomy, you should recognize these signs and take action immediately (Erwin-Toth & Doughty, 1992).

At times, you may be able to manage a blockage yourself. A warm bath to relax the muscles along with peristomal massage may help to dislodge the plug. Replacing the current appliance with one that has a larger opening could reduce the swelling. If you're not vomiting, fluids may help. But be aware, that if these conservative measures don't work, you must seek medical help.

A blockage can become a serious medical emergency if ignored. If you have any of the following symptoms, you must act immediately. The stool stops completely and you have cramps, nausea and/or vomiting. Without fluid replacement you can develop an electrolyte imbalance, and you need medical attention (Erwin-Toth & Doughty, 1992).

When you have an ileostomy, you can lose between 16 to 26 ounces of fluid in the stool daily. Failure to replace fluids can lead to a severe fluid and electrolyte imbalance. Signs of the problem include the following:

1. Dry mouth,
2. Low blood pressure,
3. Decreased urine output and increased urine concentration,
4. Weakness,
5. Muscle cramps,
6. Fatigue,
7. Confusion, and
8. Nausea and vomiting.

It is imperative for those with ileostomies to replace fluids, or they may become quickly dehydrated. At all times, ileostomates must monitor the status of their fluids (Erwin-Toth & Doughty, 1992).

Colostomy Concerns

The location of the surgery on the large intestine will determine any special situations that you might encounter with a colostomy. Those who have had surgery in the ascending colon face many of the same issues as those with an ileostomy. People with transverse colostomies must increase fluids, but don't face a great risk of blockages. Prolapse is more often an issue due to the large size of the stoma. If you have a descending or sigmoid colostomy, the greatest risk is constipation. Preventative measures include adequate fluids, fiber, and exercise. If you have a colostomy and do not pass stool in 24 hours, or have hard stool or abdominal swelling, you need to seek medical advice. Most of the time, a stool softener or laxative will help, but there is a potential danger of a colostomy obstruction, and you should monitor bowel status on a regular basis to avoid that issue (Erwin-Toth & Doughty, 1992).

Urostomy Concerns

The major potential complications of urostomies are urinary tract infection and stone formation. Adequate fluids are key to preventing these problems. Signs of an infection are

1. Cloudy urine with a strong odor,
2. Changes in the urine pH,
3. Fever,
4. Nausea and vomiting,
5. Anuria (lack of urine production).

You must recognize these signs so that appropriate treatment can begin. Proper fluids and hygiene reduce the risk of these complications, and regular visits to your urologist to monitor the upper urinary tract are essential (Erwin-Toth & Doughty, 1992).

Stone formation is a problem that can occur due to chronic urinary tract infections, alkaline urine, and concentrated urine. Plenty of fluids are the best defense against this problem. Some dietary changes may be needed and a few of your favorite foods may have to be eliminated, as the goal of the urostomate is to have dilute and acidic urine. A degree in chemistry is not required to meet this goal since appropriate fluids will meet the body's requirements for proper balance (Erwin-Toth & Doughty, 1992).

As you can see, there are some potential health risks and concerns when traveling with an ostomy. If you follow the rules of good dietary habits and get adequate fluids, many of the issues can be avoided. Most importantly, don't be afraid to seek medical help when needed.

Appendix 1:

How can I obtain ostomy information and management guidelines during my travels?

In The United States and Canada:

The United Ostomy Association, Inc. (UOA) provides information about local chapters throughout the United States.
UOA
19772 MacArthur Blvd.
Suite 200
Irvine, CA 92612-2408
Telephone: (949) 660-8624 or 1 (800) 826-0826 (toll free)
Fax: (949) 660-9262
Website: www.uoa.org

The United Ostomy Association of Canada, Inc. provides information about local chapters throughout Canada.
UOA of Canada, Inc.
P.O. Box 825
50 Charles Street East
Toronto, ON M4Y 2N7
Telephone: (416) 595-5452 or
1(888) 969-9698 (toll free)
Fax: (416) 595-9924
e-mail: uoacan@total.net

World Wide:
The International Ostomy Association (IOA) is an association of worldwide ostomy associations. The website address is: www.ostomyinternational.org.

IOA Regional Associations and telephone numbers: European Ostomy Associations

Algeria	213 321-15-21
Austria	43 1 332 3862
Belgium	32 3 15-61 48 60
Bulgaria	359 2 80 64 71
Croatia	385 1 377 85 10
Czech Republic	420 543248517
Denmark	45 57 67 35 25
Egypt	20 2 258 1958
Finland	358 31 2140 989
France	331-45 57 40 02
Germany	49 81 61 93 43 01
Greece	30 1-6 43 08 11
Hungary	36 82 427971
Israel	972 3-5 71 72 34
Italy	39 2 36 02 74170 63 57 71
Latvia	371 7 36 63 51
Lebanon	961 3-5 71 72 34
Luxembourg	352 370 150
The Netherlands	31 34 62-6 22 86
Norway	47 22-46 10 10
Poland	48 618 21 9301
Portugal	351 1 8596054
Republic Belarus	7 0172 69-62 13169 62 11
Romania	40 64 16 17 12
Russia	7 095 299 9401
Slovak Republic	421 842 36 519
Slovenia	386 62 225 223
Spain	34 1-3 08 41 86
Sweden	46 19-17 00 50151
Ukraine	7 44 225 40 56
United Kingdom	44 1189 391537
Yugoslavia	99 381 21 61 5711Ext.432

Asian Ostomy Associations

China	86 21 5347081 78009
Hong Kong, China	852 2834 6096
India	91 22 4 12 80 87
Japan	81 3-5670-7681
Korea	82 2 275 4771
Malaysia	(603) 707 5359

| Singapore | 65 2 21 95 77 |
| Thailand | 662 246 0061 Ext.286 |

North and Central America and Caribbean Ostomy Associations

Bermuda	441-236-4163
Canada	1 888 964-9698 (toll free)
Costa Rica	506 438 0832
Dominican Republic	809 565 6489
Mexico	52 5 662 1525
Panama	507-2-63 0598
Puerto Rico	787 762 3314
United States	1(800) 826-0826

South American Ostomy Associations

Argentina	54 1 983 7335
Bolivia	591 3 337555
Brazil	55 21 252 5702
Chile	56 2 226 1497
Colombia	571 6 307 917
Ecuador	593 4 293 459
Peru	51 14 499137
Uruguay	598 3 85 6697

South Pacific Ostomy Associations

| Australia | 61 2 4957 1820 |
| New Zealand | 64 3 454 5330 |

African Ostomy Associations

Cameroon	237 22 50 84
Iraq	964 60 771097
Seychelles	248 225 376
South Africa	27 423 962 261
Zimbabwe	263 4 70 55 22

REGIONAL OSTOMY ASSOCIATION CONTACT INFORMATION

ASIA:

CHINA
Ostomy Association of China
Chang Hai Hospital
174 Chang Hai Road
Shanghai
China 200433
Telephone: 86 21 5347018 78009
Fax: 86 21 65492727

INDIA
OAI (Ostomy Association of India)
74 Jerbai Wadia Road
Bhoiwada
Parel, Mumbai 400 012
India
Telephone: 91 22 4 12 80 87
Fax: 91 22 1 16 56 38
e-mail:
ostomy@bom.3.vsnl.net.in

INDIA
India Ostomy Society
c/o Institute Rotary Cancer Hospital
A.I.I.M.S. Ansari Nagar
New Delhi -110 029
India
Telephone: 91 11 6431352, 6432132

IRAQ
Mosul Ostomy Unit
Mosul Cancer Control Committee
Mosul Teaching Hospital
P.O. Box 760
Mosul
Iraq
Telephone: 964 60 771097 or 610254

JAPAN
Japan Ostomy Association Inc.
1-1-1-901 Higashi-Shinkoiwa
Katsushika-ku
Tokyo 124
Japan
Telephone: 81 3-5670-7681
Fax: 81 3-5670-7682

KOREA
Korea Ostomy Association
(Sung San Buid 503 Ho)
20-14 6KA Eulcciro
Jung Ku
Seoul 100-196
Korea
Telephone: 82 2 275 4771

MALAYSIA
Stoma Care Society of Malaysia
190 Jalan C3 Taman Melawati
53100 Kuala Lumpur
Malaysia
Telephone: 60 3 408 1653
e-mail:

axon@tm.net.my

PHILIPPINES
Philippines Cancer Society, Inc.
310 San Rafael Street
San Miguel
P.O. Box 3066
1005 Manila
Philippines
e-mail:
pcsi@uplink.com.ph

SINGAPORE
Stoma Club of Singapore
15 Engor Street 04-01
to 04 Realty Centre
Singapore 079716
Telephone: 65 2 21 95 77
Fax: 65 2 22 74 24

THAILAND
Thailand Ostomy Foundation
c/o National Cancer Institute
268.1 Rama 6 Road
Thoong Phayathai
Rajthevi
Bangkok 10400
Thailand
Telephone: 662 246 0061 Ext. 286
Fax: 662 246 5145

LATIN AMERICA:

ARGENTINA
Liga Argentina Colostomia Ileostomia Urgstomia
L.A.C.I.U.

Casilla De Correo 1560
1000 Buenos Aires
Argentina
Telephone/Fax: 54 17 92 80 95

Asociacion Argentina de Ostomizados
Casilla de Correo 42 Suc 24
1424 Buenos Aires
Argentina
Telephone: 54 1 983 7335
Fax: 54 1 901 1410

BOLIVIA
Asociacion Boliviana de Ostomizados
Casilla de Correo 318
Santa Cruz de La Sierra
Bolivia
Telephone: 591 3 337555

BRAZIL
Sociedade Brasileira dos Ostomizados
Rua Republica do Libano
35/Centro
Rio de Janeiro
RJ/CEP-20.061-030
Brazil
Telephone: (021) 252 5702/509-6846
Fax: (021) 252 5702
e-mail:
sbo@olimpo.com.br

CHILE
Corporation de Ostomizados de Chile

Santa Monica No 2278
Santiago Centro
Chile
Telephone/Fax: 56 2 226
1497

COLUMBIA
Ostomizados de Valle de
Cauca (O.V.A.)
Apartado Aereo 011419
Cali
Colombia
Telephone: 571 23
6612431

Association Colombiana
de Ostomizados
Calle 67 B No.55-16
Santa Fé de Bogotá
D.C.,
Colombia - Sur América
Telephone: 571 6 307
917 or 57 918 427 771
Fax: 571 4 168 355
e-mail: m_acero@hot-
mail.com

ECUADOR
Asociacion Ecuatoriana
de Ostomizdos
(A.E.D.O.)
P.O. Box 09-01-4877
Guayaquil
Ecuador
Telephone: 593 4 293
459
Fax: 593 4 286 911 /
593 4 454 168

PERU
Asociacion de Ostomiza-
dos del Peru
Angamos Este 2520

Surquillo 34
Lima
Peru
Telephone: 51 14
499137
Fax: 51 14 490064

URUGUAY
Asociacion Uruguaya de
Ostomizados
Pinos M12 S20, Solymar
(1005) Depto.
Canelones
Uruguay
Telephone: 598 3 85 66
97

VENEZUELA
Asociacion Venezolana
de Ostomizados
P.O. Box 62.268
Chacao
Caracas 1060
Venezuela
Telephone: 58 2 51 59
35
Fax: 58 2 51 59 08

EUROPE:
ALGERIA
Algerian Ostomy Associ-
ation
Clinique Mohamed
Boudiaf
12 Rue Kesri Amar
Tizi-Ouzou
Algeria
Telephone: 213 321-15-
21
Fax: 213 321-79 60

AUSTRIA

Osterreichische ILCO
Ileostomie, Colostomie,
Urostomie - Vereingung
Obere Augartenstr 26-28
A - 1020 Vienna
Austria
Telephone/Fax: 01 332 38 63

BELGIUM
Stoma Club Antwerpen
Ooststatiestraat 163
B2550 Kontich
Belgium
Telephone/Fax: 32 3 459 82 85

Stoma Club Liege
34, rue Victor Carpentier
B-4020
Liege-Bessoux
Belgium

Stoma-Ilco Belgie
Dalialaan 8
B-3191 Boortmeerbeek
Belgium
Telephone: 32 3 15-61 48 60

BULGARIA
Bulgarian Ostomy Association
Christo Belchev Str 21
Sofia 1000
Bulgaria
Telephone/Fax: 359 2 80 64 71

CROATIA
CRO-ILCO

Ilica 198
41000 Zagreb
Croatia
Telephone/Fax: 385 1 377 85 10

CZECH REPUBLIC
CZECH ILCO
Smidkova 5a
CZ 61600 Brno
Czech Republic
Telephone/Fax: 420 543248517

DENMARK
Stomiforeningen COPA
Odinsveg 5
DK-4100 Ringsted
Denmark
Telephone: 45 57 67 35 25
Fax: 45 57 67 35 15
e-mail:
flcopa@get2net.dk

EGYPT
Egypt Ostomy Association
One Roxy Square 304
Helipolis
Cairo 1161
Egypt
Telephone: 010 1415211 or 202 2581958
Fax: 202 588 5132
e-mail: BSEgypt@compuserve.com

FINLAND
FINNILCO RY
P.O. Box 242
SF-33101 Tampere

Finland
Telephone: 358 31 2140 989
Fax: 358 31 2127 981
e-mail: finnilco@finnilco.fi
Website: www.finnilco.fi

FRANCE
Federation des Stomises de France
76 rue Balard
F-75015 Paris
France
Telephone: 331-45 57 40 02
Fax: 331-45 57 29 26
Website: www.fsf.asso.fr

GERMANY
Deutsche ILCO
Landshuter Str. 30, D-85356 Freising,
Postfach 1265, D-85312 Freising
Germany
Telephone: 49 81 61 93 43 01 or 93 43 02
Fax: 49 81 61 93 43 04
e-mail: info@ilco.de
Website: www.ilco.de

GREECE
ILCO Greece
c/o Hellenic Anticancer Institute
171 Alexandrae Avenue
GR-603 Athens 115-22
Greece
Telephone: 30 1-6 43 08 11
Fax: 30 1-6 42 01 46

HUNGARY
Hungarian ILCO Association
Szente Imre u. 14
H-7401 Kaposvar
Hungary
Telephone/Fax: 36 82 427971
Website:
www.surgi.dote.hu/ilco/
or
www.surgi.dote.hu/ilco/indea/htm (English)

ICELAND
ISILCO
Skogarhlid 8
IS-101
Reykjavik
Iceland

ISRAEL
Israel Ostomy Association
c/o Israel Cancer Association
P.O.B. 437
Givataim 53104
Israel
Telephone: 972 3-5 71 72 34
Fax: 972 3-5 71 95 78
e-mail:
isoa@eshnav.com
Website:
eshnav.com.isoa/

ITALY
A.I. STOM
Via Venezian 1
1-20133 Milano
Italy
Telephone: 39 2 36 02

74/70 63 57 71
Fax: 39 2 239 0508

LATVIA
ILCO-Latvia
Bruninieku iela 5
Riga LV-1100l
Latvia
Telephone: 371 7 36 63
51 or 31 51 74
Fax: 371 7 31 32 73

LEBANON
Lebanese Ostomy Association
P.O. Box 166378
Saint George's Hospital
Beyrouth
Lebanon
Telephone: 961 1
581714
Fax: 961 1 582560
e-mail:
mdaher@lb.refer.org

LITHUANIA
LiSA Lithuanian Stoma
Patients Associations
Josvaniu g.2
Kaunas 3021
Kaunas Medical Academy
Lithuania

LUXEMBOURG
ILCOLUX
51 Rue du Centre
L-3960 Enlange/Mess
Luxembourg
Telephone: 352 370 150

THE NETHERLANDS
Nederlandse Stomavereniging "Harry

Bacon"
Wilhelminastraat 45
NL-3621 VG Breukelen
The Netherlands
Telephone: 31 34 62-6
22 86
Fax: 31 34 62-5 03 56
e-mail:
harrybacon@tip.nl
Website:
www.harry-bacon.nl

NORWAY
NORILCO
Fr.Nansens vei 12
Postboks 5327
Majorstua
N-0304 OSLO
Norway
Telephone: 47 22-46 10
10
Fax: 47 22-60 69 80

POLAND
POL-ILKO
Zarzad Glowny
ul. Przbyszewkiego 49
60-355 Poznan
Poland
Telephone: 48 618 21
9301
Fax: 48 42 30 31 26

PORTUGAL
A.P.O (Association Portugesa de Ostomizados)
Ava Joao Paulo 11
Zona J de Chelas
Lote 552 2 B
P-1900 Lisbon
Portugal
Telephone/Fax: 351 1
8596054

Liga de Ostomizados de Portugal
Estrada da Circunvalacao, 8881
4200 Porto
Portugal
Telephone: 351 2 830 0525

REPUBLIC BELARUS
BELSA
Proctology Dept.
District Clinical Hospital
223052 MINSK - Lesnoy-1
Republic Belarus
Telephone: 7 0172 69-62 13/69 62 11
Fax: 7 0172 66 555 2

ROMANIA
Romanian Ostomy Association
Str. Plo Pilor Nr. 18 Ct 3, ap 7
3400 CLUJ - NAPOCA
Romania
Telephone: 40 64 16 17 12
Fax: 40 64 19 30 38

RUSSIA
Moscow Regional Public Organization of Ostomy Patients, "ASTOM"
Strastnoi Bulvard, 15/29-10
103006 Moscow
Russia
Telephone/Fax: 7 095 299 9401

ASSCOL, Russia Ostomy Association
1st Liniya 48
199053 St. Petersburg
Russia
Telephone/Fax: 7812 213 55 18

Republic Kalmykia-Halmg Tangch
(Contact Address only)
Kalmyk Ostomy Association
358000 ELISTA
Gorky Street 35/36
Republic Kalmykia-Halmg Tangch

SLOVAK Republic
SLOVILCO-SLOVAK OSTOMY ASSOCIATION
Ing.Stefan Pindroch
Hurbanova 23
SK-036 01 Martom
Slovak Republic
Telephone: 421 842 36 519

SPAIN
AEDO (Asociacion Espanola de Ostomizados)
42 Dpdo 4
28010 Madrid
Spain
Telephone: 34 1-3 08 41 86

SWEDEN
ILCO Sweden Ostomy Association
Box 81 35

S-700 08 Orebro
Sweden
Telephone: 46 019 170050
Fax: 46 019 170052
e-mail: mail@ilco-for-bundet.se

SWITZERLAND
ILCO Schweiz
IM Neuacher 2
5454 Bellikon
Switzerland

UKRAINE
ILCO Ukraine
Kiev Healthcare Department
17 Shevchenko Avenue
Kiev 252030
Ukraine
Telephone: 7 44 225 40 56
Fax: 7 44 224 16 09

UNITED KINGDOM
British Colostomy Association
15 Station Road
Reading
Berkshire, RG1 1LG
England
United Kingdom
Telephone: 44 1189 391537
Fax: 44 1189 569095
e-mail: sue@bcass.org.uk
Website: www.bcass.org.uk

The Ileostomy and Internal Pouch Support Group
P. O. Box 132
Scunthorpe
DN159YW
United Kingdom
Telephone: 44 01724 720150
Fax: 01724 721601
e-mail: ia@ileostomy-pouch.demon.co.uk
Website: www.ileostomypouch.demon.co.uk

Urostomy Association
Beaumont Park
DANBURY
Essex, CM3 4DE
England
United Kingdom
Telephone/Fax: 44 1245 227569

N.A.S.P.C.S.
(National Association for Support of Parents of Children with Stomas)
51 Anderson Drive
Valley View Park
Darvel
Ayrshire
Scotland, KA17 ODE
United Kingdom
Telephone: 44 15603 22024
e-mail: john@stoma.freeserve.co.uk

YUGOSLAVIA
Stoma Society of Vojvodina

21000 Novi Sad
Omladinskog Pokreta 11
Yugoslavia
Telephone: 99 381 21 61
5711 Ext. 432 or 564
Fax: 99 381 21 61 5741

AFRICA:

CAMEROON
Central Hospital,
Yaounde
P.O. Box 8189
Yaounde
Cameroon
Telephone: 237 22 50 84
Fax: 237 20 79 47

SEYCHELLES
Liaison Unit of Non Governmental Organization
P.O. Box 885
Victoria, Mahe
Republic of Seychelles
Telephone: 248 225 376
Fax: 248 225 379

SOUTH AFRICA
Ostomy Association of
Southern Africa
P.O. Box 1398
Jeffreys Bay
6330 South Africa
Telephone: 27 423 962
261
Fax: 27 423 931 095

ZIMBABWE
The Ostomy Association
of Zimbabwe
Cancer Association of
Zimbabwe
P. O. Box 3358

Harare
Zimbabwe
Telephone: 263 4 70 55
22

Ostomy Clinic, The Cancer Centre
60 Livingstone Avenue
Harare
Zimbabwe
Telephone: 263 4 72 17
88

NORTH, CENTRAL AMERICA AND CARIBBEAN:

BERMUDA
Ostomy Association of
Bermuda
P.O. Box 2281
Hamilton HMJX
Bermuda
Telephone: 441-236-4163

CANADA
UOA CANADA, Inc.
P. O. Box 46057
College Park Post Office
Toronto, ON M5B 2L8
Canada
Telephone: 1 888 964-
9698 (Toll Free)
Telephone: 416 595 5452
Fax: 416 595 9924
e-mail:
uoacan@astral.magic.ca
Website: www3.ns.sympatico.ca/canada.ostomy/

COSTA RICA
Associacion Pro Ayuda Al
Ostomizado

Apartado Postal 11832-
1000,
San Jose,
Costa Rica
Telephone/Fax: 506 438
0832

DOMINICAN REPUB-
LIC
Dominican Ostomy Asso-
ciation
Hector Garcia Godey #
35
Arroyo Hondo
Santo Domingo
Dominican Republic
Telephone: 809 565 6489
Fax: 809 687 7410

MEXICO
Ostomizados Unidos de la
Ciudad de
Mexico A.C.
Alfonso Esparza Oteo
139-12
Colonia Guadalupe Inn
Mexico D.F.01020
Mexico
Telephone: 52 5 662 1525
Fax: 52 5 663 4213

THE NETHERLANDS
ANTILLES
STOMA VERENISINS
NEDERLANDSE
ANTILLEN
R.O.S.A.
P.O. Box 4697
Curacao
The Netherlands Antilles

PANAMA
Asociacion Panamena de
Ostomizados
Apto 5856, Zona 3
Panama
Republic de Panama
Telephone: 507-2-63
0598
Fax: 597-2-63 4370

PUERTO RICO
Asociacion de Ostomiza-
dos de Puerto Rico
P.O. Box 9332
Plaza Carolina Station
Carolina,
Puerto Rico 00988-9332
Telephone: 787 7623314
e-mail:
aopr@geocities.com
Website:
www.geocities.com/hot-
springs/villa/3721

UNITED STATES
United Ostomy Associa-
tion
19772 MacArthur Boule-
vard
Suite 200
Irvine CA 92612-2405
U.S.A.
Telephone: 949 660-8624
Fax: 949 660-9262
e-mail: uoa@deltanet.com
Website: www.uoa.org

Appendix 2:

How can I locate a surgeon who specializes in Colon and Rectal Surgery?

The American Society of Colon and Rectal Surgeons (ASCRS) maintains a listing of board certified colorectal surgeons (Fellows) as well as surgeons who hold a membership in the society (Members). These surgeons can be found in each of the United States, Washington DC and Puerto Rico.

The following countries are also represented with surgeons who are members of ASCRS:

Argentina	Australia	Austria
Belgium	Bolivia	Brazil
Canada	Chile	China
Colombia	Czechoslovakia	Denmark
Egypt	France	Germany
Greece	Guatemala	Hong Kong
India	Iran	Iraq
Ireland	Israel	Italy
Japan	Jordan	Korea
Lebanon	Malaysia	Mexico
New Zealand	Norway	Panama
Peru	Philippines	Poland
Portugal	PR China	Rep Georgia
Saudi Arabia	Scotland	Singapore
Spain	Sri Lanka	Sweden
Switzerland	Taiwan	The Netherlands
Turkey	United Kingdom	Uruguay
Venezuela	Viet Nam	Wales

Each listed surgeon with ASCRS has an address and telephone number. Most have FAX numbers and many have e-mail addresses. Prior to travel, contact the American Society of Colon and Rectal Surgeons to locate surgeons in the geographic region of interest.

American Society of Colon and Rectal Surgeons
 85 West Algonquin Road
 Suite 550
 Arlington Heights, IL60005
 (847) 290-9184
 Fax: (847) 290-9203
 e-mail: ascrs@fascrs.org
 Website: www.fascrs.org

Appendix 3:

How can I locate an enterostomal therapist?
Enterostomal therapy nurses (ETs) can be contacted
several ways:

World Council of Enterostomal Therapists (an inter-
national association of nurses)
Box 48099
60 Dundas Street East
Mississauga, Ontario, Canada L5A4G8
Telephone: (905) 848-9400
Fax: (905) 848-9413
e-mail: wcet@on.aibn.com

Wound, Ostomy and Continence Nurses Society (an
association of ET nurses)
1550 South Coast Highway
Suite 201
Laguna Beach, CA92651
Telephone: (888) 224-WCON (toll free)
Fax (949) 376-3456
Website: www.wocn.org

Other ways to locate an ET nurse:

Contact a member of the American Society of Colon
and Rectal Surgeons in the region of your travel for
an ET referral. [See Appendix 2]

Contact the United Ostomy Association (UOA) or the
International Ostomy Association (IOA) for a referral.
[See Appendix 1]

Appendix 4:

How can I obtain ostomy supplies during my travels?
One way to obtain information about distribution of ostomy supplies is to contact the International Ostomy Association (IOA) which has worldwide sites, listed in Appendix 1.

The following is a sample of telephone numbers and addresses for suppliers in North America.
Addresses and telephone numbers were accurate at the time of printing.

Cambridge Neutraceuticals
1 Liberty Sq., Boston, MA 02109
800-265-2202

Carrington Laboratories
PO Box 168128, Irving, TX 75016
800-358-5205

Coloplast/Sween
PO Box 8300 N, Mankato, MN 56002
800-788-0293 or (800) 237-4555

ConvaTec
100 Headquarters Pk. Dr., Skillman, NJ 08558
800-422-8811

ConvaTec
555 Dr. Frederick Phillips, Suite 110, Montréal (Québec) H4M 2X4
800-465-6302

Cymed
1336A Channing Way, Berkeley, CA 94702
800-582-0707

Dansac, Inc
307-A S Westgate Dr., Greensboro, NC 27407
800-538-0890

Gentel 800-840-9041

Hollister, Inc
2000 Hollister Dr., Libertyville, IL 60048
800-323-4060

Marlen
5150 Richmond Rd., Bedford, OH 44146
216-292-7060

Nu-Hope Laboratories
PO Box 31150, Pacoima, CA 91333
818-899-7711
800-899-5017

Ostomy USA
800-846-5994

Rystan Co., Inc
PO Box 214, Little Falls,
NJ 07424
201-256-3737

Smith & Nephew United
11775 Starkey Rd,
Largo, FL 34649
800-876-1970

Torbot Group
PO Box 6008, Warwick,
RI 02887 800-545-4254

VPI
127 S. Main St., Box
266 Spencer, IN 47460
800-843-4851

The Perma-Type Co
83 Northwest Dr.,
Plainville, CT 06062
800-243-4234

DISTRIBUTORS
The following is a sample of telephone numbers and addresses for distributors in North America.
Addresses and telephone numbers were accurate at the time of printing.

Marc Ostomy & Surgical
6200 Wilshire Blvd., Los
Angeles, CA 90048
213-938-7131

Medical Care Products
PO Box 10239, Jacksonville, FL 32247
800-741-0110

A-1 Home Health Care
2915 Ingersoll Ave., Des
Moines, IA 50312
800-373-9500

Hammer Medical
523 E Grand Ave., Des
Moines, IA 50309
800-388-1187

Keefer Drug/Ostomy
5 West Prospect Ave.,
Mount Prospect, IL
60056
847-255-3220

Hospital Drug Store
200 Loyola Ave., New
Orleans, LA 70112
800-256-2007

Ostomy Care Center
102 West 39th St.,
Kansas City, MO 64111
816-753-6446

Williams Surgical Supp
1501 Church St.,
Nashville, TN 37203
800-422-8811

Byram Healthcare Center
75 Holly Hill Lane,
Greenwich, CT 06830
800-354-4054

Med-Equip Ostomy
305 East Fifth St., Canton, SD 57103
800-462-4109

Bruce Medical
PO Box 9166, Waltham,
MA 02254
800-225-8446

American Ostomy Supply
PO Box 13396, Milwaukee, WI 53213
800-858-5858

AARP Pharmacy Service
PO Box 14899, Fort
Worth, TX 76117
800-284-4788

EdgePark Surgical
2300 Edison Blvd.,
Twinsburg, OH 44087
800-321-0591

Blain Maclean Surgical
3407 26th Ave. SW, Calgary, Alberta, CN
T3EON3
403-249-7515

Congdons Aids
15819
Stony Plain Rd.,
Edmonton, Alberta, CN
T5P3Z7
800-252-9368

Homecare & Surgical
11044 82nd Ave.,
Edmonton, Alberta, CN
T6G0T2
800-272-8851

Market Drugs Medical
10203 97th St., Edmonton, Alberta, CN
T5JOL5
800-282-3913

Ostomy Care & Supply
2004 Eighth Ave., New
Westminster, BC, CN
V3M2T5
604-522-4265

Contact Information for
Manufacturers and Distributors World Wide
Addresses and telephone numbers were
accurate at the time of
printing.

ARGENTINA
ConvaTec
Monroe 825 Planta Baja
Capital Federal (1428)
Buenos Aires,
ARGENTINA
Telephone: (54 1) 789-8400

Abbott Laboratories
Argentina, S.A.
Casilla de Correo N.
5196
Correo Central 1000
Buenos Aires, Argentina
Telephone: (54)
13829341
Fax: (54) 13829441

AUSTRALIA
ConvaTec—A Division
of Bristol-Myers Squibb
Australia Pty Ltd
PO Box 240
Noble Park, Victoria
3174
Telephone:(03) 9554-9400 or 1 800 335 276
Fax: (03) 9554-9443

Liberty Medical Pty., Ltd.
9 Central Blvd.,
Port Melbourne, Victoria 3207, Australia
Telephone: (61) 396464033
Fax: (61) 396464018

AUSTRIA
Bristol-Myers Squibb Ges.m.b.H, ConvaTec-Division
Columbusgasse 4
A-1100 Wien, Austria
Telephone:0660-633979

BAHRAIN
Al-Jishi Corporation W.L.L.
P.O. Box 617, Salmaniya Avenue, Manama,
State of Bahrain
Telephone (973) 233544
Fax: (973) 255602

BANGLADESH
ConvaTec Bangladesh c.o Kapricorn Enterprise
62/2, Purana Paltan
Dhaka - 1000
Bangladesh
Telephone: (880) 2955-6660 / 1 / 2

BELGIUM
ConvaTec, A Bristol-Myers Squibb Co.
Waterloo Office Park
Building J
Dreve Richelle
161, B 23/24

B-1410 Waterloo Belgium
Telephone: (32-2) 352-7200

Hollister Belgium
52 Chaussée des Collines
1300 Wavre, Belgium
Telephone: (32) 10230470
Fax: (32) 10230488

BOLIVIA
Importadora Fernando Seoane 167 Casilla N 5
Santa Cruz, Bolivia
Telephone: (59) 13336762
Fax: (59) 13325019

BRAZIL
ConvaTec, Uma Companhia Bristol-Myers Squibb Brasil SA
Rua Carlos Gomes, 924
S-o Paulo SP, Brazil
04743-903
Telephone: (55-11) 882-2000 or (outside of Brazil) 0800-115-115

Hollister de Brazil, Ltd.
Avenida Nova Independencia, 956 CEP 04570-001
Brooklin Novo, Sao Paulo, SP, Brazil
Telephone: (55) 1155066550
Fax: (55) 1155064988

BULGARIA RSR
27B Tsar Ivan Shishman
1000 Sofia, Bulgaria
Telephone: 3592 980
9971

CHILE
ConvaTec, Una Compa-
nia de Bristol-Myers
Squibb
Avenida Presidente
Balmaceda 2168
Santiago, Chile
Telephone: (562) 672-
1564

Laura Care, Ltd.
Dr. Agustin Andrades
4395 Nunoa
Santiago de Chile, Chile
Telephone: (56)
22713367
Fax: (56) 22713367

CHINA
Bristol-Myers Squibb
Shanghai
9/F Shanghai Broadcast-
ing & TV Tower
No. 651 Nan Jing Road
West
Shanghai 200041
China
Telephone: (86-21) 6255
3138

COLOMBIA
ConvaTec, Une Compa-
nia de Bristol-Myers
Squibb
Sucursal de Colombia
Calle 34 No. 6-06
Bogota, Colombia
Telephone:(571) 285-
1188 or (571) 232-8020
or (Toll Free) 9800-
10034

Bioquimicos de Colom-
bia, Ltd.
Calle 39 a nro 17-43/47
Santa Fe de Bogota,
Colombia
Telephone: (57)
12459880
Fax: (57) 12881745

COSTA RICA
ConvaTec-Bristol-Myers
Squibb, Contiguo a
Siemens
La Uruca
San Jose, Costa Rica
Telephone: (506) 257-
5278

San Jose Medica
P.O. Box 878-2150
San Jose, Costa Rica
Telephone: (506)
2409370
Fax: (506) 2409370

CROATIA
Stoma Medical d o o
Savska 41 /XIX
41000 Zagreb
Croatia
Telephone: (385) 1 612-
1640

CURACAU
Obudar Agencies
Julianaplein #42
Williamstad, Curacau
Telephone: 011-599-
961-5011

CYPRUS
Cyprus Pharmaceutical
Organization, Ltd.
Papaellina House, 35
King Paul I St.
P.O. Box 1005
Nicosia 136, Cyprus
Telephone: (357)
2443141
Fax: (357) 2365136

CZECH REPUBLIC
ConvaTec s.r.o.
Lazarska 6
12000 Praha
Czech Republic
Telephone: 420 22101
6111

Glynn Brothers Chemi-
cals, spol. s.r.o.
Na Safránce 28, 10100
Praha 10, Czech Repub-
lic
Telephone: (42)
267311892
Fax: (42) 267312922

DENMARK
ConvaTec Information
J3/4gersborgvej 64-66
2800 Lyngby
Denmark
Telephone: 45 87 60 11

Hollister Denmark
P.O. Box 1211 Lille
Kongevej
DK-3480 Fredensborg,
Denmark
Telephone: (45)
48465100 or (Toll Free)
8030-6011

Fax: (45) 48465110

**DOMINICAN REPUB-
LIC**
ConvaTec, Bristol-Myers
Dominicana
Autopista 30 de Mayo
Km. 13 1/2
Santo Domingo, Repub-
lica Dominicana
Telephone: (809) 537-
0050

DoMed del Caribe, S.A.
Calle David Ben Gurion
Esq
Fredy Prestol Castillo
No 5A Ensanche Pianti-
ni
Santo Domingo, Repub-
lica Dominicana
Telephone: (809) 472-
4108 or (809) 472-4307
Fax: (809) 567-9395

ECUADOR
ConvaTec, A Bristol-
Myers Squibb Co.
Av. Las Americas
Edificio Mecanos, Piso 3
Guayaquil, Ecuador
Telephone: 593
4289043 or 593
4289063

Monica Carrion
Guayacanes Mz., 233-A
Villa 12
Guayaquil, Ecudaor
Telephone: (593)
4823060
Fax: (593) 4284157

EGYPT
ConvaTec Middle East
1, Wadi El Nil Street
Mohandessin
P.O. Box 223, Guiza
(12211)
Cairo, Egypt
Telephone: (202) 303-1890

International Import &
Export Center
24 Tripoli St. from
Abass El-Akkad St.
6th Zone, Nasser City,
Cairo, Egypt
Telephone: (20) 22705892
Fax: (20) 22705893

EL SALVADOR
Bristol-Myers Squibb
Avenida Olimpica
#3765
Colonia Escalon
San Salvador, El Salvador
Telephone: (503) 224-3900

ESTONIA
BMS Estonia
Sepise 18,
Talninn 11415, Estonia
Telephone: 372
6401301

FINLAND
Oriola Oy
P.O. Box 8
Oriontie 5
SF-02101 Espoo
Finland

Telephone: (358-9)
42999

Hollister Scandinavia,
Inc.
Suomen Sivuliike Luut-
nantintie 3 D 00410
Helsinki, Finland
Telephone: (358)
95308600
Fax: (358) 953086020

FRANCE
Laboratoires ConvaTec
La Grande Arche Nord
92044 Paris La Défense
cedex
France
Telephone: 0800 35 84
80 or (Service Informa-
tion Toll Free): 05 35 84
80

Hollister
92 Avenue d'Lena
75116 Paris, France
Telephone: (33)
147237210
Fax: (33) 147235855

GERMANY
ConvaTec Vertriebs-
GmbH
Ein Unternehmen der
Bristol-Myers Squibb
Gruppe
Volkartstrasse 83
D-80636 München
089-12142-0
Telephone: 0800 -
7866200
Wundversorgung
Telephone: 01802-21 21

24
Inkontinenzversorgung
Telephone: 01802-67 21
80

Hollister Incorporated
Niederlassung Deutsch-
land
Postfach 1323 Münchn-
er
Strasse 16 85774
Unterföhring, Germany
Telephone: (49)
899928860
Fax: (49) 8999288645

GREECE
ConvaTec, A Bristol-
Myers Squibb Co.
357-359 Messoghion
Avenue
152 31 Chalandri,
Greece
Telephone: (30-1) 6501-
582/4

Remek S.A.
P.O. Box 65100
58 Katehaki St.
15410 Psihiko
Athens, Greece
Telephone: (30)
16755832
Fax: (30) 16713708

GUATEMALA
Humana S.A.
2 de Avenida, 3-43 Zona
10,
Guatemala City,
Guatemala
Telephone: (502)
2346040

Fax: (502) 2346041

HONDURAS
Tecnomedic S.A.
7 Avenida 4 y 5 Calle
Barrio El Benque Edifi-
cio Fuazo Castro
San Pedro Sula, Hon-
duras
Telephone: (504)
579025
Fax: (504) 578994

HONG KONG
ConvaTec Pacific Region
Unit D., 16/F, Manulife
Tower
169 Electric Road
North Point, HONG
KONG
Telephone: (852) 2510
6500

Y.C. Woo & Co., Ltd.
Rooms 402-404, Wing
Shan Tower
173 Des Voeux Rd. Cen-
tral,
Hong Kong
Telephone: (852)
25217304
Fax: (852) 28684312

HUNGARY
Pharmavit Rt
A Bristol-Myers Squibb
Co.
Veresegyhaz, Levai utca
5
2112 Hungary
Telephone: 36 28 385
960

ICELAND
Pharmaco hf
Postholf 200
Horgatuni 2
PO Box 200
IS-212 Gardabaer
Iceland
Telephone: 354 56 58
111
Fax: 354 56 56 485

INDIA
ConvaTec
Fleet Building
Marol Naka, Sir M.V.
Road
Andheri (East) Bombay
400059
India
Telephone: (91) 22-852-
2629 / 852-2638

S-Three Sales Interna-
tional Pvt. Ltd.
398 Masjid Moth, South
Extension Part II
New Delhi, 110 049,
India
Telephone: 011-625
0301
Fax: 011-625 0103

INDONESIA
ConvaTec Indonesia
c/o P.T. Enseval Putera
Megatrading
Enseval Building, 4th
Floor
Jl. Jetjen, Suprapto
Jakarta Pusat, Indonesia
Telephone: (62-21) 424-
3908

IRELAND
ConvaTec
St. John's Court
Unit 3, Block 2
Santry, Dublin 9
EIRE
Telephone: 1800
721721(Toll Free Help
Line)

Hollister Limited
Belgard Road, Tallaght
Dublin 24, Ireland
Telephone: (353)
14041680
Fax: (353) 14041682

ISRAEL
Philtel Ltd. 14 Shenkar
str. Kiryat Arie 49513
P.O. Box 3918
Petach Tikva 49130
Telephone: (972) 1-800-
800-150 (Toll Free)

Promedico, Ltd.
4 Baltimore Street
Kiryat Arieh Petach-
Tikva, Israel
Telephone: (972)
39265965
Fax: (972) 39248548

ITALY
ConvaTec, Divisione
della Bristol-Myers
Squibb S.P.A
Via Paolo di Dono, 73
00143 Roma
Italia
Telephone: (39-6) 503-
961

Hollister S.P.A.
Strada 4, Palazzo A/8
20090 Milanoflori Assa-
go
Milanofiori, Italy
Telephone: (39)
028228181
Fax: 0039/02/57518377

JAMAICA
Medi-Grace
33 1/2 Eastwood Pk. Rd.
Kingston, Jamaica

JAPAN
ConvaTec Division, Bris-
tol-Myers Squibb K.K.
27F Shinjuku i-Land
Tower
6-5-1 Nishi-shinjuku, 6-
chome
Shinjuku-ku, Tokyo 163-
13 Japan
Telephone: (81-3) 5323-
8461

Hollister Company Lim-
ited
Ohno Takanawa Bldg.,
7th Floor 2-21-38
Takanawa, Minato-Ku
Tokyo 108, Japan
Telephone: (81)
332806200
Fax: (81) 3-3280-6430

JORDAN
Kawar Drug Stores
P.O. Box 922025
Amman, JORDAN
Telephone: (9026) 606-
512 / 3

Bio-Jordan Est
P.O. Box 850251
Amman 11185, Jordan
Telephone: (962)
65512612
Fax: (962) 65515612

KOREA
ConvaTec Korea c/o
Zimmer Korea
17th floor, Sung-won
Building
141, Samsung-dong,
Kangnam-Ku,
Seoul, Korea
Telephone: (82-2) 3453-
6333
Fax: (82-2) 3453-6335

KUWAIT
Yusuf Ibrahim Al Ghan-
im & Sons
P.O. Box 435
13005 Safat
Kuwait
Telephone: (965) 483-
3608

Abdul Aziz Yousuf Al-
Essa & Co., W.L.L.
P.O. Box 3562, Safat
13036
Safat Kuwait
Telephone: (965)
4833051 or (965)
4833065 or (965)
4833075
Fax: (965) 4840629

LEBANON
Khalil Fattal & Fills
S.A.L.
P.O. Box 773

Sin El Fil - Jisr El Wati
Beirut, Lebanon
Telephone: (961-1)
425450

MACEDONIA
T P Panovski
67 Leninova Street
91000 Skopje
Macedonia
Telephone: 389 91 222 -
813

MALAYSIA
ConvaTec North Pacific
c/o Bristol-Myers Squibb
(M) Sdn Bhd
Lot 1839, Jalan Gergaji
15/14
40000 Shah Alam
Selangor, Malaysia
Telephone: (60-3) 550-
7995

Inchcape Waleta SDN
BHD
46400 Petaling Jaya
Selangor Darul Ehsan,
Malaysia
Telephone: (60)
37682299
Fax: (60) 37549939

MALTA
ConvaTec
Tibet Onorato Bres St.
Ta'xoieux MSD II
Malta
Telephone: 356-33-44-
12

MEXICO
E.R. Squibb & Sons de
Mexico
Avenida Revolucion No.
1267
Col. Tlacopac, Delga-
cion
A. Obregon
01040 Mexico D.F.
Telephone: 91-800-00-
885(Toll Free) or (525)
6-64-44-59

Hollister S.A. de C.V.
Privada Ignacio Vallarta
#13, Piso 1-2. Col.
Tabacalera, C.P. 06040
 Mexico D.F., Mexico
Telephone: (52)
55926338 or (52)
55926368
Fax: (52) 55926303

NETHERLANDS
ConvaTec
Vijzelmolenlaan 9
3447 GX WOERDEN
The Netherlands
Telephone: for Osto-
my&Continence Care
0800-0224444
for Wound & Skin Care
0800-0224460

Hollister BV
Maanlander 25
3824 MN Amersfoort,
Netherlands
Telephone: (31)
334501000
Fax: (31) 334501001

NEW ZEALAND
ConvaTec—A Division
of Bristol-Myers Squibb
(New Zealand) Ltd.
PO Box 14-445
Panmure, AUCKLAND
Telephone: (09) 573
1166 or 0800 441 763
(Toll Free)
Fax: (09) 573 1174

Hollister Limited
49 George Street, P.O.
Box 4079 Newmarket,
Auckland, New Zealand
Telephone: (64) 9 377
3336
Fax: (64) 9 307 1307

NICARAGUA
Refanic
Del Arbolito 1 Cuadra
Abajo 1 Cuadra Allago
Managua, Nicaragua
Telephone: (505) 266-
3916

Casa Teran S.A.
Edificio Teran Calle
Momotombo #888
Managua, Nicaragua
Telephone: (505) 228
5000
Fax: (505) 2283088

NORWAY
ConvaTec Informasjon
Norge
Postboks 490
N-1323 HOVIK
Norway
Telephone: 800 30995
(Toll Free)

Hollister Norge
Ullernchausséen 119
P.O. Box 166 Lilleaker
N-0216
Oslo, Norway
Telephone: (47) 22 511
900
Fax: (47) 22 511 905

OMAN
Muscat Pharmacy
P.O. Box 438
P C 113
Muscat, Oman
Telephone:(968) 771
4501 or (968) 771 4502
Fax: (968) 771 5201

Ebin Rushed Pharmacy
Co., L.L.C.
P.O. Box 169
Muscat, Sultanate of
Oman
Telephone: (968)
701557 or (968) 701567
or (968) 796218
Fax: (968) 701547

PAKISTAN
Squibb Pakistan Ltd.
ConvaTec
B-105, Mohammad Ali
Housing Society
Tipu Sultan Road
Karachi, Pakistan
Telephone: (92-21) 453-
0586 / 7

Iqbal Enterprise
B/24-25, 2nd Floor
Zeenat Medicine Mar-
ket, Denso Hall
Karachi, Pakistan

Telephone: (92)
214525293
Fax: (92) 214525294

PANAMA
Bristol-Myers Squibb,
ConvaTec Panama Ofici-
na Regional
Avenida Cuba y Calle 39
Panama Republica de
Panama
Telephone: (50) 737-
3177

Panama Medical
Edificio Marbella Torre
S.B.
P.O. Box 6-1014
Panama, Republica de
Panama
Telephone: (507)
233988
Fax: (507) 694938

PERU
Atilio Palmieri S.R.L.
Av. Salaverry 2409 Block
Posterior 2415, of 401
Lima 27, Peru
Telephone: (51)
14422452
Fax: (51) 14445248

PHILIPPINES
ConvaTec Philippines
Room 603, 6th floor,
Culmat Bldg.
127-133 E. Rodriguez
Sr. Avenue
Corner 12th Street,
Quezon City
Philippines
Telephone: (63-2) 721-
1103

POLAND
Bristol Myers Squibb sp
zoo
Globe Trade Center-
SATURN BUILDING
ul Domaniewska 41
02-672 Warszawa
Poland
Telephone: 00-48-22-
874-38-10

PORTUGAL
ConvaTec, Uma divis-o
da Bristol-Myers Squibb
Farmacutica Portogue-
sa,Lda.
Edificio Fern-o de Mag-
alh-es
Quinta da Fonte
2780 Porto Salvo
Portugal
Telephone: (351-1) 440
70 70 or 0800-20-1678
(Toll Free)

Medicinália
Rua de Proletariado
Quinta de Paizinho P-
2795
Carnaxide, Portugal
Telephone: (351)
14247300
Fax: (351) 14176484

PUERTO RICO
Squibb Corporation of
Puerto Rico, ConvaTec
Division
#6 Tabonuco Street
Caparra Hills Develop-
ment
Guaynabo, Puerto Rico
00968
Telephone: (787) 792-
3780

Puerto Rico Hospital
Supply, Inc.
Ave. Rosendo Vela Acosta Lote 4 Jardines
Industriales de Carolina
Carolina, 00987, Puerto
Rico
Telephone: (809)
2575151
Fax: (809) 2575105

QUATAR
Gentech Gulf Engineering & Technical Services
P.O. Box 8960, Granada
Building
Doha, Qatar
Telephone: (974)
868100
Fax: (974) 866445

ROMANIA
Pharmavit Rt, A Bristol-Myers Squibb Co.
Veresegyhaz, Levai utca
5
2112 Hungary
Telephone: 36 28 385
960

RUSSIA
Bristol-Myers Squibb
Russia
Trekhprudny per 7-9
Stronie 1b
103001 Moscow
RUSSIA
Telephone: (70 95) 755-9267

SAUDI ARABIA
Salehiya Establishment

P.O. Box 3869
Jeddah 21481
Saudi Arabia
Telephone: (96 61) 463-4364

Farouk, Maamoun,
Tamer & Company
P.O. Box 180 Jeddah
21411
Saudi Arabia
Telephone: (966)
26435600
Fax: (966) 26439834

SERBIA
TT Medik
Bulevar Lenjina 10D/1
ENJUB Centar
11070 Novi Beograd
Serbia
Telephone: (381) 11-222-1142

SINGAPORE
Bristol Myers Asia/Pacific Inc.
Pasir Panjang Distri
Park
Block 1 #02-16
Pasir Panjang Road
Singapore, 0511
Telephone: 65-276-7663

Summit Co. (Singapore)
Pte., Ltd.
396 Alexandra Road,
#12-00 BP Tower,
Singapore 119954
Telephone: (65)
2739988
Fax: (65) 2787011

SLOVAKIA
Pharmavit Slovakia
Klariska 7
81103 Bratislavia
Slovakia
Telephone: (427) 531
8502

SLOVENIA
Valencia Stoma Medical
Zupancieceva 10
61000 Ljubljana
Slovenia
Telephone: (386) 61-
214-959

SOUTH AFRICA
ConvaTec Division, Bristol-Myers Squibb
PO Box 643
47 van Buuren Road
Bedfordview 2008
South Africa
Telephone: (27-11) 456-
6500

Hollister South Africa
(Pty.), Ltd.
Lechwe Street Corporate Park
Midrand, Private Bag
X116
Halfway House 1685,
South Africa
Telephone: (27)
113142505
Fax: (27) 113142506

SOUTH KOREA
Chung-Ang Instrument
Co.
C.P.O. Box 249.
Seoul, South Korea

Telephone: (82)
25776451 or (82)
25776456
Fax: (82) 25776457

SPAIN
ConvaTec, S.A., Grupo
Bristol-Myers Squibb
Edificio Diagonal II,
Bloque A, 4a planta
08960 Sant Just Desvern
(Barcelona)
España
Telephone: 93 371 07
00 or 900 30 40 50 (Toll
Free)
Fax: 93 372 46 52

Hollister Ibérica, S.A.
Calle Caleruega, 81
Planta 3-Oficina A
28033
Madrid, Spain
Telephone: (34)
913838727
Fax: (34) 917669201

SRI LANKA
ConvaTec Sri Lanka,
Muller and Phipps (ceylon) Ltd
P.O. Box 117
4th Floor York Arcade
Building
8-4/2 Leyden Bastian
Road
Colomo 1
Sri Lanka
Telephone: (94-1) 422-
382 / 437-132

264

Akbar Pharmaceuticals
(Pvt.), Limited
P.O. Box 1726, No. 334
T.B. Jayah Mawatha
Colombo 10, Sri Lanka
Telephone: (94)
1697151 or (94)
1695541
Fax: (94) 1699029

SWEDEN
ConvaTec/Bristol-Myers
Squibb
Box 15200
Gustauslundsvagen 145
S-161 15,
Bromma, Sweden
Telephone: 020-21 22
22

Hollister Sverige
Enhagsslingan 5 187 40
Taby, Sweden
Telephone: (46)
84464646
Fax: (46) 84464645

SWITZERLAND
Bristol Myers Squibb
AG, ConvaTec Division
Neuhofstrasse 6
6341 Baar
Switzerland
GebYhrenfreier Telefon-
service: 0800 55 11 10
Telephone: (41-41) 767-
72 00

Hollister Incorporated
Niederlassung Deutsch-
land c/o Globopharm
AG
Gewerbestrasse 12 CH-

8132
Egg, Switzerland
Telephone: (41)
19844540
Fax: (41) 19844542

TAIWAN
ConvaTec Taiwan
c/o Bristol Myers Squibb
Taiwan
4th Floor, C.D.C. Tower
125 Nanking E. Road,
Section 5
Taipei, Taiwan
Telephone: (886-2) 756
1280

Enfield Medical Co.,
Ltd.
Floor 16, No. 57 Fuhs-
ing North Road
Taipei, Taiwan, Republic
of China
Telephone: 886-2-8773-
4261
Fax: 886-2-8773-4262

THAILAND
ConvaTec Thailand c/o
Diethelm & Co. Ltd.
Pharmaceutical Division
280 New Road
Bangkok, 10100, Thai-
land
Telephone: (66-2) 226-
6545

Inter Medical Co., Ltd.
999/99 V.A.T. Building
Rama 9 Road, Suanlu-
ang
Bangkok 10250, Thai-
land

Telephone: (66)
27183333
Fax: (66) 27183588

TURKEY
BMS International, Inc.
Istanbul Subesi
Yapi Kredi Plaza
B Blok Kat 10
Levent
80620 Istanbul, Turkey

Hekimsan Medikal Limited Sirketi
Suleyman Sirri Sokak
21/2 Sihhye
Ankara, Turkey
Telephone: (90)
3124357446
Fax: (90) 3124359778

UNITED ARAB EMIRATES
United Arab Emirates
(90-212) 270-9165
U.A.E. City Pharmacy
P.O. Box 2098
Abu Dhabi, United Arab
Emirates
Telephone: (9712) 732-521 / 730-790

Al-Razi Pharmaceuticals
Co.
P. O. Box 285
Abu Dhabi, United Arab
Emirates
Telephone: (971)
2341745 or (971)
2326671
Fax: (971) 2339451
Dubai Office P.O. Box
19790

Dhabi, United Arab
Emirates
Telephone: (971)
4217761
Fax: (971) 4211460

UKRAINE
Bristol Myers Squibb sp
zoo
Globe Trade Center-
SATURN BUILDING
ul Domaniewska 41
02-672 Warszawa,
Poland
Telephone: 00-48-22-
874-38-10

UNITED KINGDOM
ConvaTec Ltd.
Customer Service
Harrington House
Milton Road
Ickenham, Uxbridge
UB10 8PU England
Telephone: 0800
289738 (Toll Free Help
Line)

Hollister Europe Limited
Rectory Court 42 Broad
Street
Workingham, Berkshire
RG40 1AB, England
Telephone: (44)
1189895063, (44)
1189895000
Fax: (44) 1189895046 or
(44) 1189775881

URUGUAY
Sanyfico S.R.L.
Av. 8 de Octubre 2573
Montevideo, Uruguay
Telephone: (598)
2470716
Fax: (598) 2476695

VENEZUELA
ConvaTec, a Bristol-
Myers Squibb Co.
Calle Bernardette
Edif. Bristol-Myers
Squibb
Los Cortijos De Lourdes
Caracas, DF, Venezuela
Telephone: (582) 283-
3811 / 239-5122 or 800-
69377 (Toll Free)

Distribuidora Medica
Paris, S.A.
Edificio Medica Paris
Gran Avenida (Plaza
Venezuela) Apartado
60681
Caracas 1060-A,
Venezuela
Telephone: (58)
27819045
Fax: (58) 27931753

VIETNAM
YTECO Medical
Import-Export Co
181 Nguyen Dinh Chieu
Street
Ho Chi Minh City, Viet-
nam
Telephone: (84-8) 225-
986 or (84-8) 292-014

Appendix 5a

English to Dutch, German, French, Italian, Norwegian
Adapted from the Stomawoordenboek in 11 Europese talen, Nederlandese Stomavereniging "Harry Bacon"

ENGLISH Types of Ostomy	DUTCH Soorten Stoma's	GERMAN Stomaarten	FRENCH Types de Stomie	ITALIAN Species da Stoma	NORWEGIAN Stomityper
Stoma, ostomy	stoma	stoma, anus praeter	stomie	stomia	stomi
Colostomy	colostoma (dikke darmstoma)	colostomie	colostomie	colostomia	colostomi
Ileostomy	ileostoma (dunne darmstoma)	ileostomie	ileostomie	ileostomia	ileostomi
Urostomy	urinestoma	urostomie	ureterostomie	urostomia	urostomi
Kock's pouch	continent stoma	Koksche tasche	poche de Kock	tasca di Koch	Kock's reservoir
Pouch, reservoir	reservoir	pouch	poche, reservoir	tasca, sacca	reservoir

Ostomy Appliances	Stoma-opvangmateriaal	Stoma Versorgungsartikel	Appareillage por Stomises	Apparecchiatura per stomia	Stomiutstyr
Bag, pouch	zakje	beutel	poche	sacca	pose
Adhesive bag	plakzakje	klebebeutel	poche adhesive	sacca adhesiva	pose med klebeflate
Drainable bag	alfvoerzak	austreifbeutel	poche vidangeable	sacca di drenaggio	tombar pose

ENGLISH	DUTCH	GERMAN	FRENCH	ITALIAN	NORWEGIAN
Urostomy bag	urinestoma-zakje	urostomiebeutel	poche por uterostomie	sadda di urostomia	urotomipose
Stoma cap	stoma cap	stomakappe	stoma cap	sacca post irrgazione	stomihette
One-piece appliance	een-delig systeem	einteilige versorgung	systeme monobioc	sacca monouso	endeld-bandasje
Two-piece appliance	twee-delig systeem	zweiteilige versorgung	systeme deux pieces	sistema a due pezzi	to-delt-bandasje
Flange	huidplaat	basisplatte	protecteur cutane	flangia	koblingsring
Flexible flange	flexibele huidplaat	flexible basisplatte	protecteur cutane souple	flangia flessibiletry	kkavlastende krage
Microporous adhesive area	microporeuze rand	mikroporose klebeflache	surface adhesive micropore	superficie adhesiva mocroporos	mikroporost plaster
Size of ring	maat van de ring	ringgrosse	diametre de l'anneau	diametro del foro	ringstorrelse
Size of ostomy	stomagrootte	stomagrosse	diametre de la stomie	diametro della stomia	stomidiameter
Filter	filter	filter	filtre	filtro	filter
Night bag	nachtzak	nachtbeutel	poche de nuit	sacca da notte	nattpose
Belt	riem	gurtel	ceinture	cintura	belte
Fastener clips for bags	afsluitklem	beutelclamp-verschlussklammern	molette	poseklips	
Covers for bags	hosejes	beuteluberzuge	couvre-poche	copri sacca	posetrekk
Irrigation system	spoelsysteem	irrigations-set	appareil d'irrigation	set per irrigazione	irrigasjons-sett
Catheter	catheter	katheter	catheter	catetere	kateter

ENGLISH	DUTCH	GERMAN	FRENCH	ITALIAN	NORWEGIAN
Accessories	Toebehoren	Zubehor	Accessoires	Accessori	Hjelpemidler
Skin-barrier	huidbescherming	hautschutz	protecteur cutane	protezione cutanea	kudbeskyttelse
Karaya-skin protection	karaya huidbescherming	karaya-hautschutz	karaya protecteur cutane	protezione cutanea con karaya	karaya ring
Stomahesive skin protection	Stomahesive-huidbescherming	stomahesive-hautshutz	stomahesive protecteur cutane	protezione cutanea con stomahesive	stomskin plate
Skin-barrier plate	huidbeschermings-plaat	hautschutzplatte	protecteur cutane	flangia protezione cutanea	hud plate
Cream	crème	crème	pommade	crema, ungento	krem
Gel	gel	gel	gel	gel	gele
Paste	oasta	paste	pate	pasta	pasta
Powder	poeder	puder	poudre	polvere	pulver
Lotion	lotion	lotion	lction	lotione	hud vann
Seal rings	aandrukringen	abdichtringe	anneau d'etancheite	il foro da attacare	tetningsring
Wipes	compressen	kompressen	compresses	compressa	kompresser
Cleaning agent	reinigingsvloeistof	reinigungsmittel	necessaire de nettoyage	salvietta igneica	hudrensemiddel
Deodorants	deodorants	deodorantien	deodorarts	deodorante	lukt-fjerner
Cotton wool	watten	watte	coton	ovatta	vatt
Soap	zeep	seife	savon	sapone	sape
Scissors	schaar	schere	ciseaux	forbiuci	saks

ENGLISH	DUTCH	GERMAN	FRENCH	ITALIAN	NORWEGIAN
Medical Terms	Medische termen	Medizinische Begriffe	Termes Medicaux Medicinale	Expressione	Medisinske uttrykk
Bowel, intestine	darm	darm	intestin	intestino	tarm
Anus	anus	after, anus	anus	ano	endetarmsapning
Large bowel, colon	dikke darm	dickdarm	gros intestin, colon	grosso intestino (colon)	tykktarm, colon
Small intestine	dunne darm	dunndarm	intestin grele	piccolo intestino (duedeno-ileo)	tynntarm, ileum
Kidney	nier	niere	rein	rene	nyre
Bladder	blaas	blasé	vessie	vescica	urinblaere
Ureter	ureter	harnleiter	uretre	escada de urina	urinor
Cancer	kanker	krebs	cancer	carcinoma, cancro	kreft
Crohn's disease	ziekte van Crohn	morbus Crohn	maladie de Crohn	morbo di Crohn	Crohn's sykdom
Ulcerative colitis	colitis ulcerosa	colitis ulcerosa	recto-colite ulcerohemorragique	colite ulcerosa	ulceros colitt
Familiar polyposis	familaire polyposis coli	familiare polyposis	polypose familiare	poliposi familiare	familiaer polypose
Inflammation	onsteking	entzundung	inflammation	inflammazione	betennelse
Disease, sickness, illness	ziekte	krankheit	maladie	malattia patoligica	sykdom
Handicap, disability	handicap	behinderung	handicap	handicap	funksjonshemming
Operation, surgery	operatie	operation	operation, intervention, chirurgicale	intervento chirurgico	operasjon
Complications	complicaties	komplikationen	complications	complicanze	komplikasjoner
Prolapse	prolaps (uitstulping)	prolaps	prolapsus	prolasso	prolaps, fremfall

ENGLISH	DUTCH	GERMAN	FRENCH	ITALIAN	NORWEGIAN
Hernia	hernia, breuk	hernie, bruch	hernie	ernia	brokk
Fistula	fistel	fistel	fistule	fistola	fistel
Retraction	retractie (instulping)	retraktion	retraction	retrazione	retraksjon, tilbake trekking
Stenosis	stenose (afsluiting)	stenose	stenose	stenosi	stenose, forsnevring
Abscess	abces	abszess	abces	abscesso	byll
Skin irritation	huid-irritatie	hautenzundung	inflammation de la peau	inflammazione hud-(irritazione) della pelle	irritasjon
Skin problems	huidproblemen	hautprobleme	probleme de peau	problemi cutanei	hud problemer
Allergy	allergie	allergie	allergie	allergia	allergi
Leaky, not tight	niet-afgesloten (lekkage)	undicht	pas etanche	non attaca	lekkasje
Diarrhea	diarree	durchfall	diarrhee	diarrea	diare
Constipation	obstipatie (verstopping)	verstopfung	constipation	stipsi	forstoppelse
Stool	onlasting	stuhl	selles	feci	avforing
Urine	urine	urin	urine	urine	urin
Bandage	bandage	bandage	bandage	bandage	bandasje
Equipment	**Uitrusting, voorzieningen**	**Ausstattung**	**Equipment**	**Equipaggiamento**	**Utstyr**
Toilet, lavatory	toilet, wc	toilette, wc	toilettes, cabinets, wc	wc, gabinetto	toalett, wc
Wash room, lavatory	badkamer	waschraum	lavabo	lavandino	vaskerom, skyllerom
Shower	douche	dusche	douche	doccia	dusj

ENGLISH	DUTCH	GERMAN	FRENCH	ITALIAN	NORWEGIAN
Bathroom	badkamer	bad	salle de bains	sali da bagno	bad
Bath tub	badkuip	badewanne	baignoire	il bagno	badekar
Water	water	wasser	eau	acqua	vann
Mineral water	mineraalwater	mineralwasser	eau minerale	acqua minerale	mineralvann
Toilet paper	toiletpapier	toilettenpapier	papier hygenique	carta igenica	toalettpapir
Dust bin, waste basket	afvalemmer	abfalleimer	seau a ordures, poubelle	secchio di avanzi	soppelkurv
Professionals	**Deskundigen**	**Fachleute**	**Specialistes**	**Specialistas**	**Spesialister**
Physician, doctor	dokter, arts	arzt	medecin, docteur	il medico, il dottore	doktor
Internist, internal specialist	internist	internist	specialiste des maladies	internes internisto	indermedisiner
Surgeon	chirurg	chirurg	chirurgien	chirurgo	kirug
Urologist	uroloog	urologe	urologue	urologo	urolog
Pharmacy, chemist's shop	apotheek	apotheke	pharmacie	la farmacia	apotek
Medical supply shop	medische specialzaak	sanitatshaus versorgung smitelgschaft	maison de sante, maison de cure	studio medico	forretning for syke pleiearthkler
Bandagist, orthopedic technician	bandagist	bandagist orthopadietechniker	bandagiste	dendaggio, tenico otropedico	bandagist
Ostomy therapist	stomaverpleeg-kundige	stoma therapeut/in	stomatherapeute	stomaterapista, enderomista	stomaterapeut
Hospital	ziekenhuis	krankenhaus	hopital	ospedale	sykehus

ENGLISH	DUTCH	GERMAN	FRENCH	ITALIAN	NORWEGIAN
Medicine, medication	medicijnen geneesmiddelen	medikamenta	remede, medicament	farmaco, medicamento	Medisinske uttrykk
Account, bill	rekening	rechnugg	facture	conto	regning
Sick-fund, health insurance company	ziekenfonds, ziektekosten-verzekeraar	krankenkasse	caisse de maladie	servizio sanitario nazionale	trygdekasse
International sick certificate	internationale ziektekaart	int krankenschein	bulletin international de maladie, feuille internationale d'assurance maladie	certificato internazionale di malattia	reiseforsikring
Assurance, insurance company	verzekering	versicherung	assurance	assiurazione	forsikring
Embassy	ambassade	botschaft	ambassade	ambasciata	ambassade
Ambassador	ambassadeur	botschafter	ambassadeur	ambasciatore	ambassador

Appendix 5b

English to Portuguese, Serbo-Croatian, Spanish, Turkish, Swedish

ENGLISH	PORTUGUESE	SERBO-CROATIAN	SPANISH	TURKISH	SWEDISH
Types of Ostomy	**Tipos de Ostomia**	**Vrsta-stoma**	**Clases, tipos de Ostomias**	**Stoma Turleri**	**Typer af Stomier**
Stoma, ostomy	ostomia	stoma, izlas	ostomia	stoma (agiz, delik)	stomi
Colostomy	colostomia	colostomie	colostomia	kolostoma (kalin bagirsak stomasi)	colostomi
Ileostomy	ileostomia	ileostomie	ileostomia	ilyostoma (ince bagirsak stomasi)	ileostomi
Urostomy	urostomia	urostomie	urostomia	urinestoma (idrar stomasi)	urostomi
Kock's pouch	bolsa de Kock	Kozk Dzep	reservorio de Kock	altini tutabilme stomasi	Kock's reservoar
Pouch, reservoir	bolsa, reservatorio	rezervoar	reservorio	hazne	Backen reservoar
Ostomy Appliances	**Aparalhagem**	**Artikili koji**	**Dispositivos para pripadaju stomi**	**Stoma-toplama Ostomias**	**Stomiatiklar malzemesi**
Bag, pouch	bolsa, saco	vreca ili kesa	la bolsa	torba	pase

ENGLISH	PORTUGUESE	SERBO-CROATIAN	SPANISH	TURKISH	SWEDISH
Adhesive bag	bolsa adhesiva	kesa koja se iljepi	bolsa adhesiva	yapisan torba	gummi pase
Drainable bag	bolsa de drenagem	kesa za istiskivanje	bolsa drenable	atik torbasi	tombar pase
Urostomy bag	bolsa de urostomia	kesa za urinaru stomu	bolda para urostomias	idrar stomasi torbasi	urostomi pase
Stoma cap	tampas protectoras	poklopak (kapa) za stomu	tapon para ostomia	stoma basligi	stoma cap
One-piece appliance	aparelho de 1 peca	jednokratna upotreba	aplicacion de una pieza	tek bolumlu sistem	endels bandage
Two-piece appliance	aparelho de 2 pecas	dvokratna upotreba	aplicacion de dos piezas	iki bolumlu sistem	tva-dels bandage
Flange	falange	osnova ploca	placa de base	deri plakasi	blansplatta
Flexible flange	falange flexivel	fleksibilna ploca	placa de base flexible	esnek deri plakasi	flexibel platte
Microporous adhesive area	adhesivo microporoso	mikroporozna Ljepljiva Povrsina	cinta adhesiva microporosa	cok kucuk gozenekli kenar	mikroporos hafta
Size of ring	tamanho do anel	kao prsten velika	tamano o diametro de anillo	halka	ringstoriek
Size of ostomy	tamanho da ostomia	velicine stome (otvora)	tamano del ostomia	stoma buyuklugu	stomi storlek
Filter	filtro	filter	filtro	suzgek filitre	filter
Night bag	bolsa de noite	nocna kesa	bolsa para la noche	gece torbasi	natt pase
Belt	cinto	kais	cinturon, cinto	kemer	baite
Fastener clips for bags	ganchos	kesa sa klemama za zakljucavanje (spajanje)	broche, cierre	mandal, kapama kiskaci	pasias
Covers for bags	coberturas	dodatna kesa preko stome	cubrebolsa	kiliflar	yterpase

ENGLISH	PORTUGUESE	SERBO-CROATIAN	SPANISH	TURKISH	SWEDISH
Irrigation system	aparelho de irtigacao	set za irigaciju	juego para irrigacion sistemi/lavman sistemi	calkalama	irrigations system
Catheter	cateter	kateter	cateter	sonda	kateter
Accessories	**Accessorios**	**Dodaci**	**Accessorios**	**Eklentiler**	**Tillbehor**
Skin-barrier	protectores cutaneos	kozna zastita	protector de la piel	deri korunmasi	hud kram
Karaya-skin protection	karaya protectores cutaneos	karaya kozna zastita	proteccion de karaya para piel	karaya cilt korunmasi	karaya-gummi
Stomahesive skin protection	stomahesive protectores cutaneos	stomahesive kozna zastita	proteccion de stomahesive para piel	stomahesive-deri korunmasi	stomahesive-hudskydd
Skin-barrier plate	falange protectores cutaneos	poklopak (kapa) za stomu	placa protectora de la piel	deri koruma plakasi	skydds platta
Cream	crème	crème	crema	krem	salva
Gel	gel	gel	gel	jel	gel
Paste	pasta	paste	pasta	macun	pasta
Powder	po	puder	polvo	pudra	puder
Lotion	locao	lotion	solucion, locion	losyon	hudkram
Seal rings	aneis	kolutovi za dihtovanje	aros selladores de proteccion	kapama halkalan	tatnungstring
Wipes	pincas	komprese	compresa	kompresyon yapma, basma, sikistirma	kompressor
Cleaning agent	produto de limpeza	sredstva za ciscenje	elementos de limpieza temizleme sivisi		rengoringsmedel
Deodorants	desodorizantes	deo	desodorantes	deodorantlar	deodorant

ENGLISH	PORTUGUESE	SERBO-CROATIAN	SPANISH	TURKISH	SWEDISH
Cotton wool	algodao	vata	algodon	hidrofil pamuk	bumull
Soap	sabao	sapun	jabon	sabun	tval
Scissors	tesoura	makaze	tijera	makas	sax
Medical Terms	**Termos Medicos**	**Medicinski izrazi**	**Expresiones medicinales**	**Tibbi terimler**	**Medicinska termer**
Bowel, intestine	intestino	crijevo (cevo)	intestino	bagirsak	tarm
Anus	anus	anus	ano	anus/makat	andtarm
Large bowel, colon	intestino grosso	debelo crijevo	colon o intestino grueso	kalin bagirsak	tjocktarm
Small intestine	intestino delgado	tanko crijevo	ileon o intestino delgado	ince bagirsak	tunntarm
Kidney	rim	bubreb-bubrezi	riñon	bobrek	njure
Bladder	bexiga	mokracni mjehur	vejiga	kese	blasa
Ureter	ureter	mokracvod	conducto de orina, ureter	ureter; idrar yolu	uretar
Cancer	cancro	rak	cancer	kanser	cancer
Crohn's disease	doenca de Crohn	morbus Crohn	enfermedad de Crohn	Crohn hastaligi kismi ileitis	Crohns sjukdom
Ulcerative colitis	colite ulcerosa	colitis ulcerosa	colitis ulcerosa	kolitis ulseroza (kalin bagirsak iltihaplanmasi)	ulceros colit
Familiar polyposis	polipose familiar	familijarna polipoza	poliposis familiar	kalitsal bagirsak polipi	familjar polypos

ENGLISH	PORTUGUESE	SERBO-CROATIAN	SPANISH	TURKISH	SWEDISH
Inflammation	inflamacao	upala	inflamacion irritacion	iltihap	inflammation
Disease, sickness, illness	doenca de Crohn	bolest	enfermedad	hastalik	sjukdom
Handicap, disability	deficiencia	ostecenje	incapacidad, minusvalia	ozur,kusur, sakatlik	handikapp
Operation, surgery	operacao	operacija	operacion, cirugia	ameliyat	operation
Complications	complicacoes	kompliacija	complicacion	komplikasyonlar	komplikationer
Prolapse	prolapso	prolaps	prolapso	sarkma, prolaps	prolaps
Hernia	hernia	hernia	hernia, eventracion	fitik	brock
Fistula	fistula	fistula	fistula	fistul	fistel
Retraction	retraccao	retrakcija	retraccion	cekilme, busulme	retraktion
Stenosis	estenose	stenoza	estenosis	darlik, stenoz	stenos
Abscess	abscesso	absces	abceso	abse, cerahat kesesi	varhard
Skin irritation	inflamacao da pele	upala koze	irritacion cutanea	derinin tahris olmasi	hud irrigation
Skin problems	problemas da pele	kozni problemi	problemas de piel	deri rahatsizlikari	hud problem
Allergy	alergia	allergija	allergia	alerji	allergi
Leaky, not tight	nao estanque	koji propusta (ne dihtuje)	no hermetico con perdida	kapali olmayan (sizinti)	lackage
Diarrhea	diarreia	proliv	diarrea	ishal	diarre
Constipation	obstipacao, prisao de ventre	zatvor (otezana stolica)	estrenimiento	kabizlik, peklik	forstoppad
Stool	fezes	stolica (praznjenje crijeva)	materia fecal, heces	diski, buyuk, abdest	avforing
Urine	urina	urin-mikraca	orina	idrar	urin

ENGLISH	PORTUGUESE	SERBO-CROATIAN	SPANISH	TURKISH	SWEDISH
Bandage	ligadusa, bandage	bandaza	vendaje	sargi bezi, yara bezi	bandage
Equipment	**Equipmento**	**Opremanje**	**Equipo**	**Donanim, kolayliklar**	**Ultristning**
Toilet, lavatory	casa de bahno, wc	wc, toalet	toilette, servicio	tuvalet	toalett
Wash room, lavatory	lavabo	praonica vesa	lavabo	banyo	tvattrum
Shower	douche	tus	ducha	dus	dusch
Bathroom	casa de banho	banja	cuarto de bano	banyo	badrum
Bath tub	banheira	kada	banera	kuvet (banyo)	badkar
Water	agua	voda	agua	suzgek filitre	vatten
Mineral water	agua mineral	mineralna voda	agua mineral	Madensuyu	mineral vatten
Toilet paper	papel higiencio	toalet papir	papel higinico	tuvalet kagidi	toalett papper
Dust bin, waste basket	caixote do lixo	kanta za smede (dubre)	balde de desperdicios	cop tenekesi	papperskorg
Professionals	**Profissionais**	**Specijalisti**	**Especialistas**	**Uzmanlar**	**Specialiser**
Physician, doctor	medico	doktor	medico, doctor	doktor, hekim	doktor
Internist, internal specialist	interno, especialista interno	internist	medico, internista	Dahiliyeci	medicinsk doktor
Surgeon	cirurgao	hirurg	cirujano	Cerra	kirurg
Urologist	urologista	urolog	urologo	urolog/bevliyeci	urolog
Pharmacy, chemist's shop	farmacia	apotehar	farmacia	Eczane	apotek
Shop for supplies	farmacia	rednja za prodaju saniteskog	ortopedia, casa de productos	sargi gereceleri satilan yer	apotek medical

ENGLISH	PORTUGUESE	SERBO-CROATIAN	SPANISH	TURKISH	SWEDISH
Bandagist, orthopedic technician	protesico, tecnico ortopedico	majstori za protetiku materjala	vendaljista tecnico en ortopedia de sanidad	Pansumanci	otroped tekniker
Ostomy therapist	estomaterapeuta	strucni savjetnik za bolesnike sa stomom	estomaterapeuta	stoma hemisiresi	stomiterapeut
Hospital	hospital	bolnica	hospital, clinica	Hastane	sjukhus
Medicine, medication	remedio, medicamento	medikamenti	medicamentos	Ilaclar	medicin
Account, bill	conta	racun	cuenta, factura	hesap, fatura	rakning
Sick-fund, health insurance company	segurance social	bolnika kasa	seguridad social	hastalik fonu, hastalik masraflan sigortacisi	forsakringskassan
International sick certificate	certificado internacional de doencas	internacionalni bolnicki list	certificato intrenational de enfermedad	ususlararasi hastalik karti	sjukingtg
Assurance, insurance company	companhia de seguros	osiguranje	seguro, compania de seguro	Sigorta	forsakrings bolag
Embassy	embaixada	konzulat	embajada	Buyukelcilik	ambassad
Ambassador	embaizador	konsul	embajador	Buyukelci	ambassador

Appendix 6:

Other Useful Information

Ostomy Quarterly Magazine
The United Ostomy Association, Inc.
19772 MacArthur Boulevard, Suite 200
Irvine, California 92612-2405
Telephone: (800) 826-0826
Website: www.uoa.org
e-mail: uoa@deltanet.com

Crohn's and Colitis Association of America
386 Park Avenue South, 17th Floor
New York, New York 10016-8804
Telephone: (212) 685-3440, (800) 932-2433
Website: www.ccfa.org
e-mail: info@ccfa.org

American Automobile Association
100 AAA Drive
Heathrow, Florida 32746-5063
Offices Located Nationwide

Medical Identification Jewelry is available from:

• Medical-ID.com
P.O. Box 50, Verbank, NY 12585
Telephone: (800) 830-0546
e-mail: MedicalID@AOL.com

• Majestic International
P.O. Box 5871
Fullerton, CA 92838
Website: www.majintl.com/medical.htm

• Custom ID Products
P.O. Box 19279, Seattle, WA 98109
Telephone: 1-800-439-8899

• ID Technology
117 Nelson Rd., Baltimore MD 21208
Website: www.id-technology.com

• MedicAlert Foundation
2323 Colorado Avenue, Turlock, California 95382-2018
Telephone: 1-800-432-5378
Fax: 209-669-2495
Website: www.Medicalert.org

• Miss Brooke's Company,
P.O. Box 558, Bryant, AR, 72089
Website: www.missbrooke.com

Useful Websites

• The Centers for Disease Control and Prevention
Travel Information—www.cdc.gov/travel

• Chicago North Suburban UOA—
www.geocities.com/Hotsprings/Spa/9630

• ConvaTec—www.ConvaTec.com

• Cymed—www.cymed-ostomy.com

• dPlanet—www.dplanet.ch/users/triwar/ostomy/
english/organizations.html

• Hollister—www.hollister.com

• International Ostomy Association—
www.ostomyinternational.org/

• The J-Pouch Group—www.j-pouch.org

• The National Institutes of Health (US)—www.nih.gov

• Ostomy Bulletin Board—www.support-group.com

• Shaz—www.geocities.com/hotsprings/spa/8089

• Stillwater/PoncaCity UOA—
http://users.hit.net/~bobbau/uoa

• StuartOnLine—a website devoted to persons with ostomies: www.stuartonline.com

• UOA of Canada—www3.ns.sympatico/canada. ostomy/

• UOA—www.uoa.org

• The Winnipeg Ostomy Association— www.pangea.ca/~woa

• The Worcester, Massachusetts Ostomy Association— http://home.att.net/~worcesterostomy

• World Ostomy Resource— www.powerup.com.au/~takkenb/OstomySites.htm

To Locate A Doctor Overseas

International Association for Medical Assistance to Travelers (IAMAT):
Homepage: www.sentex.net/~iamat/ci.html

Contact Information for IAMAT

Canada
40 Regal Road,
Guelph, Ontario
N1K 1B5
Telephone:(519) 836-0102
Fax: (519) 836-3412
e-mail: iamat@sentex.net

New Zealand
P.O. Box 5049
Christchurch 5
Fax: (643) 352-4630
email: iamat@chch.planet.org.nz

Switzerland
57 Voirets
1212 Grand-Lancy-Geneva (For written requests only)

United States
417 Center Street
Lewiston, NY 14092
Telephone: (716) 754-4883

Bibliography

Barrie, Barbara, *Second Act: Life After Colostomy and Other Adventures*. Scribner, New York, 1997.

Benirschke, Rolf, *Alive & Kicking—The True Life Story of How an NFL Star Survived Ulcerative Colitis and Ostomy Surgery*. The Firefly Press, San Diego, 1996.

Carroll, Lewis, *Alice's Adventures in Wonderland and Through the Looking Glass*. Alfred A. Knopf, Everyman's Library Children's Classics, New York, 1992.

ConvaTec, *Living with Confidence After Ileostomy Surgery*. Princeton, NJ: E.R. Squibb.

Erwin-Toth, P., & Doughty, D.B. (1992) *Principles and Procedures of Stomal Management*. In B.G. Hampton & R.A. Bryant (Eds), Ostomies and continent diversions; Nursing Management. (pp 29-103). St. Louis: Mosby.

Favreau, Ann, *The Healing Circle*, a book of inspirational poems, available from the United Ostomy Association, 19772 MacArthur Blvd., Suite 200, Irvine, CA 92612-2405.

Hampton, B.G. (1992). *Peristomal and Stomal Complications*. In B.G. Hampton, Hampton & R.A.Bryant (Eds), Ostomies and continent diversions: Nursing Management. (105-128). St. Louis: Mosby.

Krames Communications. (1997). *Living with Your Colostomy: A Guide to Self Care*. San Bruno, CA: Krames Communications.

Mullen, Barbara Dorr and McGinn, Kerry Anne, *The Ostomy Book*, Bull Publishers, Palo Alto, 1992.

Dr. Seuss (Theodor Seuss Geisel), *Oh, the Places You'll Go!*, Random House, 1990.

Nederlandse Stomavereniging "Harry Bacon," *Stoma Woordenboe*, Breukelen, Netherlands, January 1998.

Avorn, J., Monane, M., Gurwitz, JH, et al., Reduction of Bacteriuria and Pyuria after Ingestion of Cranberry Juice. JAMA. 271 (10): 751-4 1994, March 9.

Additional Information on the Benefits of Cranberries
Kerr, K.G., "Cranberry Juice and Prevention of Recurrent Urinary Tract Infection," *Lancet*, 353 (9153): 673, 1999, February 20.

Walker, EB, et al, "Cranberry Concentrate: UTI Prophylaxis," *Journal of Family Practice*, 45 (20: 167-8, August 1997.

Kuzminski, L.N. "Cranberry Juice and Urinary Tract Infections: Is There a Beneficial Relationship?" *Nutrition Reviews*, 54 (11 pt 2): 287-90, November 1996.

Tsukada, K. et al, "Cranberry Juice and its Impact on Peri-Stomal Skin Conditions for Urostomy Patients," *Ostomy Wound Management*, 40 (9): 60-2, 64, 66-68, November-December 1994.

Glossary

Portions reprinted with permission of the Canadian Ostomy Association.

Adhesion—bands of fibrous tissue, usually resulting from inflammation; act of adhering or sticking.

Anastomosis—joining together of the parts of one or more hollow organs.

Anuria—lack of urine production.

Anus—the last 4 cm (1.5 inches) of the large bowel below the rectum, forming the excretory opening or anal canal.

Appliance—pouch and accessories worn by an ostomate over the stoma to contain body wastes.

BCIR—Barnett Continent Ileostomy Reservoir.

Bladder—organ acting as a container for urine.

Bowel—the intestine; the part of the digestive tract that lies between the stomach and the anus.

Colitis—inflammation of the large bowel.

Colon—large bowel (large intestine) that stores digestive materials and absorbs water.

Colostomy—surgical opening from the colon to the surface of the abdomen to form a stoma.

Continent Ostomy—see Kock Pouch.

Continent Urostomy—surgical construction of an intra-abdominal pouch from a section of bowel for retention of urine after dysfunction or removal of the bladder.

Crohn's disease—Ileitis, regional enteritis or granulomatous disease of the bowel—inflammatory bowel disease which can penetrate the deep lining of any part of the small or large bowel and can affect the entire digestive system from mouth to anus.

Dehydration—loss of water or moisture.

Diverticulitis—inflammation or outpouching of sac arising from the bowel wall.

Electrolytes—compounds (such as salt and potassium) that maintain the body's chemical balance.

Enterostomal Therapy Nurse (ET)—a person who specializes in the care and teaching of ostomy patients.

Face Plate—see wafer.

Familial Polyposis—a rare disease that runs in families. The colon and rectum contain many polyps. Has a strong tendency toward malignancy.

Feces—bowel waste or excrement.

Fistula—abnormal opening from bowel to surface of skin, usually causing great discomfort.

Gastroenteritis—inflammation of stomach and bowel.

Hernia—abnormal bulging or extrusion of part of an organ through tissue which contains it.

Ileitis—inflammation of the small bowel.

Ileoanal—joining the small bowel to the sphincter at the anus.

Ileostomy—surgical opening from the ileum to the surface of the abdomen to form a stoma.

Ileum—lower half of the small intestine which ends at the beginning of the large intestine in the lower right part of the abdomen; small bowel.

Irrigation—flushing of the large bowel through colostomy opening (stoma).

J-Pouch—continent ileostomy.

Karaya—available as a gum, powder or paste, for protecting the skin around the stoma.

Kidneys—two organs that filter impurities from the blood and excrete them in urine.

Kidney Stone—a solid mass of inorganic material (minerals) that has formed in the kidney.

Kock Pouch—surgical technique of constructing an intra-abdominal pouch from part of the ileum, referred to as "continent ileostomy."

Malignant—cancerous, when referring to tumors.

Mucosa—mucus secreting lining of hollow organs such as the intestines.

Mucus—thick liquid secreted by the mucosa of the gastrointestinal tract.

Nitrazine paper—(litmus) paper that changes color in the presence of acid or alkaline urine.

Ostomate—a person who has had ostomy surgery.

Ostomy—surgical opening from the intestines or ureters to the surface of the abdomen to form a stoma.

Perineal—region of the body containing the sex organs and anus.

Polyps—soft tumors.

Ring Plate—see wafer.

Rectum—lower part of the intestinal tract about 15cm (6 inches) long, ending in the anus.

Stoma—surgical opening in the abdomen to allow for disposal of body wastes.

Stenosis—narrowing of a passageway.

Trauma—body injury caused by wound or shock (sometimes a cause for ostomy surgery).

Ulcerative Colitis—an inflammatory bowel disease in which ulcers form in the intestinal lining of the colon and rectum causing severe, often bloody, diarrhea.

Ureters—ducts that carry urine from the kidneys to the bladder.

Urethra—duct by which urine is discharged from the bladder.

Urine—liquid containing body wastes, secreted by the kidneys, usually stored in the bladder and discharged through the urethra.

Urine Crystals—sharp crystals that can form on a urinary stoma, or surrounding the skin. Dissolve with soaks using white vinegar and water in a 50/50 solution.

Urostomy—surgical connection (with a piece of ileum) from the ureters to the mid-abdomen to form a stoma for discharge of urine after removal or dysfunction of the bladder.

Wafer—molded plate of an ostomy pouch system. Fits against and adheres to the skin, provides attachment for pouch systems.

Index